— THE —
PRISON ANGEL

This Large Print Book carries the
Seal of Approval of N.A.V.H.

— THE —
PRISON
ANGEL

Mother Antonia's Journey
from Beverly Hills to a
Life of Service in a Mexican Jail

MARY JORDAN
AND
KEVIN SULLIVAN

Thorndike Press • Waterville, Maine

Published in 2005 by arrangement with The Penguin Press, a member of Penguin Group (USA) Inc.

Thorndike Press® Large Print Biography.

The tree indicium is a trademark of Thorndike Press.

The text of this Large Print edition is unabridged.
Other aspects of the book may vary from the original edition.

Set in 16 pt. Plantin.

Printed in the United States on permanent paper.

Library of Congress Cataloging-in-Publication Data

Jordan, Mary, 1960–
    The prison angel : Mother Antonia's journey from Beverly Hills to a life of service in a Mexican jail / by Mary Jordan and Kevin Sullivan. — Large print ed.
      p. cm.
    ISBN 0-7862-8070-0 (lg. print : hc : alk. paper)
    1. Antonia, Mother.   2. Church work with prisoners — Catholic Church.   3. Church work with prisoners — Mexico — Tijuana (Baja California).   I. Sullivan, Kevin, 1959– .
II. Title.
BX2347.8.P74J67 2005b
271′.97—dc22
    [B]   2005018761

For our parents
and for Kate and Tom

As the Founder/CEO of NAVH, the only national health agency solely devoted to those who, although not totally blind, have an eye disease which could lead to serious visual impairment, I am pleased to recognize Thorndike Press★ as one of the leading publishers in the large print field.

Founded in 1954 in San Francisco to prepare large print textbooks for partially seeing children, NAVH became the pioneer and standard setting agency in the preparation of large type.

Today, those publishers who meet our standards carry the prestigious "Seal of Approval" indicating high quality large print. We are delighted that Thorndike Press is one of the publishers whose titles meet these standards. We are also pleased to recognize the significant contribution Thorndike Press is making in this important and growing field.

Lorraine H. Marchi, L.H.D.
Founder/CEO
NAVH

★ Thorndike Press encompasses the following imprints: Thorndike, Wheeler, Walker and Large Print Press.

CONTENTS

PREFACE

In early 2002, we asked a young woman on Islas Marías, a prison in the Pacific Ocean about 100 miles off the Mexican coast, how she liked being an inmate there. She bubbled on about the beautiful ocean setting and the fresh air, and she said it was sure better than the last prison she'd been in. She had come from La Mesa prison in Tijuana, the border city across from San Diego, where she said the conditions were brutal.

"The only good thing about that place was that Irish nun," she said.

Come again?

She told us about a nun, an Irishwoman she said, who lived in a cell alongside the inmates, helping to feed and clothe them and protect them from abuse by guards.

"I miss talking to her," she said.

We wrote ourselves a note: *Find nun who lives in prison.*

A few weeks later, we stood outside the

imposing front gate of La Mesa, a fortress of twenty-five-foot walls in the middle of a downtown Tijuana neighborhood.

Mother Antonia came to greet us at the gate, a cheery little woman in a black-and-white habit.

We sat with her, and she told us about her life, about how she was raised as a well-off girl in Beverly Hills with neighbors like Spencer Tracy. (She turned out to be Irish American.) She talked about how she spent three decades as a suburban mom in Los Angeles, raising seven children.

She told us about poor people locked up for years for stealing food, about the famous drug dealers whose bullet-blasted bodies she had washed and dressed for burial. We listened, and we were hooked. Together, we have been interviewing people as journalists for more than forty years. We have interviewed presidents and rock stars, survivors of typhoons in India, and people tortured by the Taliban in Afghanistan. We had never heard a story quite like hers, a story of such powerful goodness. This was a tale that needed telling.

For starters, we wrote a story about her life that appeared on the front page of *The Washington Post* on April 10, 2002. In the weeks that followed, letters and e-mails came pouring in. People wanted to know how to help her. A gay Catholic man wrote to say his faith had been renewed by the story of how a divorced woman had not let the church's rules diminish her faith. An old boyfriend, who had not seen her since World War II scuttled their plans for a life together, saw the story and wrote to her — in care of the prison — and they talked for the first time in fifty-seven years. Kathleen Todora, a widow from Louisiana, read the story, packed her bags, and drove to Tijuana to join Mother Antonia's mission.

That response confirmed what we already knew: Mother Antonia was rare, and those whose lives are touched by hers are affected forever. She gets under your skin, and she changes you, whether it's seeing a little more humanity in a street beggar, or no longer being able to look at a Starbucks caffe latte without imagining how much better that four dollars could have been used.

This book is a work of journalism, not an "as told to" story. Mother Antonia is the first to say she isn't perfect. She has struggled with real life problems; she has known the highs of marrying for love and lows of divorce when that love dies. Suffering from poor health for a lifetime, she has

11

ignored her ailments, grabbed hold of her gifts, and used them to do extraordinary things. She is the happiest person we have ever met.

For almost three years, we have conducted hundreds of hours of interviews with Mother Antonia. We gave her a tape recorder and tapes and asked her to tell us the stories of her life. We have sat with her in the prison and in her small house nearby filled with an eclectic mix of women: inmates just leaving the prison; women receiving cancer treatments; and mothers, daughters, and girlfriends who have come long distances to visit men in prison and have no money to stay anywhere else.

We have also talked about Mother Antonia with her friends, family, bishops, inmates, guards, wardens, police chiefs, DEA agents, Army generals, and even Benjamín Arellano Félix, one of Mexico's most notorious drug traffickers. In all possible instances, we have checked and double-checked their stories with witnesses, public records, old newspaper clippings from the Library of Congress, and even in an eye-opening interview with an ultrasecret DEA informant we were introduced to only as *Comandante X.* We have been amazed at the accuracy of Mother

Antonia's memories, even those from a half-century ago. She remembered Eddie Cantor's street address from the 1930s. And she remembered it right.

People of all faiths, or of no faith, are drawn to Mother Antonia's message of inclusion. She loves the Catholic Church, but not all its rules. She wears over her heart a cross interlaced with the Star of David, a symbol of her devotion to the Jewish faith and the lesson she learned from the Holocaust as a young girl, that no one should stand by silently in the face of suffering. Some of her most generous financial supporters are Evangelical Christians in California. Mother Antonia thinks God doesn't check IDs at Heaven's gate.

In the end, this is the story of a woman who followed a dream later in life. She was fifty when she traded suburban Los Angeles for La Mesa. Mother Antonia's hope is that she will be joined by more and more women, and someday also men, who are looking for ways to give meaning to their later years. She believes that the world is full of older people with long experience who now want to help others. We think she's right. Especially since the September 11, 2001, terror attacks and all that has followed, we think more people are looking for a way to do something to make the world a little warmer.

A couple of mechanical points.

Mother Antonia is occasionally referred to in the book as Sister Antonia. It's a linguistic difference. In English, we are used to calling members of Catholic religious orders Sister. In Spanish, the more common expression is *Madre* — mother. To all her Mexican friends, she is *La Madre Antonia*. We have preserved that here, while letting English-speakers call her Sister Antonia.

When we use the authorial "we," it means that one of us, or both, saw or heard whatever is being described. It would be too distracting to write, "she said to Kevin," or, "Mary saw." We could never get away with such imprecise attribution in *The Washington Post*. But in our marriage, "we" has come to mean either or both of us. And for the sake of kindness to our readers, "we" means that here, too.

ONE

LA MADRE

A riot rages inside La Mesa state penitentiary in Tijuana, Mexico. It's Halloween night, 1994, and the twenty-five hundred convicts locked inside one of the country's most violent and overcrowded prisons are struggling, as they do every day, to live one more.

Sixteen men are locked in a block of punishment cells on the third floor. They are there for insulting guards, fighting with other prisoners, breaking the rules. They've been here for days, some for weeks. They are agitated and angry. There is never enough food in these cells, there are never enough blankets for the cold nights. It's filthy. Worst of all, visitors aren't allowed up here. No place in the prison is harsher than these fetid punishment cells, and it's never been worse than tonight. The men can hear parties for Day of the Dead ringing from homes just outside the

15

walls. It's one of Mexico's biggest days of the year, a big, happy, noisy family celebration honoring the departed. Families are together at home or in decorated graveyards filled with light and music and tequila and the hottest, sweetest bread you can imagine, and here they are, stuck in the hole.

It's too much, just too damned much. The prisoners come up with a plan. Someone calls a guard over to ask him a question. When he comes close enough, arms quickly pass through the bars and grab him, pinning him there and taking his gun and his keys. The prisoners quickly free themselves, then grab another guard and his gun, too. They tell the guards to get the hell out, then they set mattresses on fire in the cellblock and start shooting into the air out the windows.

Fearing the worst, the guards abandon their posts and shut off the electricity. Much of the prison now belongs to the inmates, and it's completely dark except for the flames rising from the top-floor windows. Outside in the crowded neighborhood of modest concrete homes that has grown up around La Mesa, people see the fire and hear the gunshots for blocks.

Police in riot gear show up. SWAT teams

assemble on the streets. Television cameras set up quickly. Mothers and girlfriends of prisoners have come running, and they are watching a small army preparing to storm the prison.

"My son, my son, what are they going to do to him?" one woman wails.

Then into the darkness comes a tiny woman in a white habit.

She has clear white skin and round cheeks, and her smile seems to start in her bright blue eyes then spread across her face until it glows. She looks so happy.

"*¡Madre! ¡Madre!*" the desperate women call out, holding out their arms and running to her.

Everyone knows her. She is Mother Antonia. She's the American sister who lives in a cell and shivers in the same cold showers as the prisoners. She calls the men *mis hijos,* my sons, and brings a mother's love to some of Mexico's most forgotten. There are rumors that she was rich once, maybe even a millionaire or a movie star. Nobody really knows exactly where she came from or why, but they know she will help them, and they know the prisoners trust her more than anybody else.

Mother Antonia was on an errand outside the prison when she heard about the trouble and has come rushing back to her adopted home, with its imposing walls and guard towers. She hears the ominous snaps and clacks of ammunition being loaded and smells the acrid fire. Terrified women mob her.

"Calm down," she says. "This is not the time to be screaming. The men can hear you in there. They're going to be all right, but you need to pray, not yell. Everything will be all right. I'm going to go inside to see your sons — my sons — right now."

The television cameras record it all and follow her as she turns and walks toward the darkened prison entrance. The warden, Jorge Alberto Duarte Castillo, is out of town. His assistant stops her at the office by the gate.

"I can't let you go in there, Mother. It's too dangerous right now."

She insists. She demands that he call her friend Duarte. She is sure he will give permission for her to go inside. It is her home and her life. She is needed in there now. He calls, and she tells Duarte she wants to talk to her *hijos* and persuade them to end the violence.

"No, Mother, you can't go in. It's too dangerous," he says on the other end of the phone.

"Jorge, you know my mission is to be in there right now," she says. "This isn't a time to back out."

Jorge Duarte knows the prisoners listen to her. He also knows that she is right, that a massacre could well be in the making; it has happened too many times before. He gives the order to let her in.

A guard unlocks the door and lets her pass.

It is black dark inside. She is alone, walking slowly down empty hallways, feeling her way along a route she knows so well. She can hear the shots and smell the smoke from upstairs. When the lights went out, some prisoners had run to their cells while others hid under tables and behind doors. Now they come out, surprised to see Mother Antonia instead of riot police.

"Mother, what are you doing in here?" one asks her.

First one, then five, then more prisoners gather around her in the darkness. They tell her that she should get out, she could be killed. Don't worry, she tells them, I'll be safe. She leads the men, mostly poor young Catholic Mexicans raised to worship God and their mothers, into the small chapel off the prison yard. She kneels and prays out loud for angels to protect everyone in the prison. Then she rises and heads out the door, an inch at a time in the darkness, toward the punishment cells.

She shuffles her feet carefully along the prison's cement floor, her outstretched hands feeling the way along the walls. Finding the stairway leading up, she realizes she is not alone in the blackness. The men have stayed with her. She doesn't know if there are five or fifty, but she feels them and hears them all around her like a human shield. She is the closest thing to heaven most of them have ever seen, this woman who brings them pillows and pure white bandages, who keeps the guards from beating them, who never stops hugging them and telling them they are loved. They call her Mother. And they are going to take a bullet rather than have *La Madre* die tonight.

She can feel the heavy black metal doors of cells as she passes them. The screams and shooting are close now, the smoke is sharp in her eyes and lungs. She calls out to the men in the punishment cells.

They are shocked to hear her.

"Don't shoot! Mother's here!" they yell.

"Mother Antonia! Get out of here. You'll be killed!" one inmate shouts. "Please, go. You'll be shot!"

She doesn't stop. She moves forward toward their voices.

"What's going on here? The whole city is terrified," she says. "Your mothers and girlfriends and children are outside crying. Please stop. There's an army out there getting ready to come in."

She tells them that if they don't put down their weapons, more children will be orphaned, including their own. Think of your parents crying at another family funeral, she pleads. Her voice is warm, convincing, and urgent, and it suddenly changes the ugly night.

The metal door to the punishment cell block opens. She can now see a bit by the light of burning mattresses. Her white clothes are singed with ash. An inmate she knows as Blackie steps forward from the shadows.

"Mother . . ."

She pushes her way inside like a running back.

"C'mon, C'mon. Give me the guns. Give me the guns right now. I'm not going to let you get hurt. I'm not going to let them hurt you and punish you. Give me the guns."

"Mother," Blackie says. "We've been up here so long they've forgotten us. The water's gone, and we're desperate."

Mother Antonia falls to her knees in the smoky hallway. She is right in front of Blackie, looking up at him with her hands held out, palms up, pleading with him.

"It's not right that you're locked up here, hungry and thirsty. We can take care of those things, but this isn't the way to do it. I will help you make it better. But first, you have to give me the guns. I beg you to put down your weapons."

"Mother," Blackie says softly, looking down at her. "As soon as we heard your voice, we dropped the guns out the window."

Mother Antonia walks Blackie downstairs to the gate, shouting to the guards and police that he is coming out, unarmed. Duarte has hurried back from Mexicali, a nearby city, and arrives at the prison just in time to see Mother Antonia and Blackie emerge from the darkened yard. They all sit in Duarte's office, and he listens to Blackie's long list of complaints. The two men agree to a settlement. Blackie promises an end to the violence. Duarte promises better conditions. The lights come back up in the prison. The riot police pack up and leave.

Mother Antonia emerges through the

prison's front gates. The mothers and wives and daughters rush to hug her close; this time their tears are from joy.

"Why were the prisoners so angry?" one television reporter shouts.

Mother Antonia turns to face the cameras.

"They just wanted to be free," she says, her white habit shining in the hot glare of the lights. "They just wanted to be free."

There is more to the story. But she knows this isn't time to tell it. For the moment, she just turns and disappears into the night, back to her cell.

She lives there, past the guards with shotguns on the wall overhead, through the sets of iron doors, down banged-up hallways under cold neon lights. Years after the riot we visit her there, to begin discovering how such a gracious woman who lived so much of her life in the comforts of suburban Los Angeles chose to live in this hard place.

She comes to greet us at the prison's main gate. Just five foot two, wearing a black-and-white habit and a crisp white veil framing her beaming face, she is a whirligig of energy and cheer.

"¿Cómo estás, mi hijo?" How are you my son, she says, hugging and kissing each guard she passes.

Visitors in the waiting area rush to her, holding out their hands to greet her: *¡Madre! ¡Madre! ¡Madre!* She has a moment for each of them, fixing them with blue eyes so luminous they almost seem lighted from within. She touches the children gently on their heads.

She turns to us, and her smile seems to give off heat.

We follow her down a few long corridors and into the heart of the prison. All around her are prisoners, a few wearing ironed shirts, clean jeans, and leather boots, but many dressed in rags. She greets every prisoner and guard she passes. She's exuberant, and everything about her says life is good, life is fun.

She sees one guard and practically shouts, "*¡Buenos días, Sergio!*"

Another can't cork his grin when she nearly sings at him, "*¡Hola, mi amor!*"

We see right away how warmly Mother Antonia touches everyone, how much she likes people. We look at the prison guards standing on the wall above her and see gruff men in knockoff Ray-Bans, the official eyewear of Third World law enforcement, and wonder what they do to prisoners when nobody is looking. She looks up all sparkly-eyed at the same

24

guards as if they are the most beautiful thing she has ever seen. She has given them a copy of the movie *The Green Mile,* dubbed in Spanish. It's about redemption, kindness, and hope, and it's set on death row. Her kind of flick. A guard tells her he loved the movie, and he's passing it on to another guard that night.

"¡Qué bueno, mi amor!" — How great, my love, she responds.

Mother Antonia's accent is pure *gringa,* as the Mexicans say. She doesn't care that she doesn't speak Spanish like Cervantes, she just plows ahead and everyone understands her. She believes that what she lacks in perfect verb conjugations, she makes up for in love for Mexico.

We arrive with her at the *Gallinero,* the Rooster House, a large cell filled with prisoners who have committed minor infractions. A couple dozen men are caged there, some standing, some lying on the concrete floor. The smell is brutal from the single toilet in the corner. Mother Antonia passes her arms through the bars and touches the men and kisses their cheeks. A few of them look hard and mean, but most of them just look sad. She asks them, "Have you eaten? Do you need anything? Is there anyone I can call for you?"

Most inmates are freely walking around the prison. To an outsider, the place doesn't look so much like a prison as a big, walled city. As we move on, Mother Antonia sees an inmate she knows. He is wearing lipstick and a dress.

"¡Mamá! ¡Mamá! ¡Mamá!" the man says to her, embracing her as if hugging his own mother. Three other transsexuals in full drag do the same. As they swish away down the narrow passageway into the crowd of inmates, Mother Antonia says that nobody has a tougher life, in the prison or outside, than they do. Not only are they struggling with their sexuality, but they don't fare too well in the prison's macho culture, so she pays them special attention.

"You love the unlovable," says Frank, a prisoner who is waiting for her at the heavy mesh door of her cell, which is only a few steps away from the holding cell for the newcomers.

"I love the people whom other people think are unlovable," she says.

Mother Antonia introduces us to Frank, a tall and muscular former U.S. Marine. Frank says he made a dumb mistake and he's learned from it, thanks to Mother Antonia. He's serving a six-year sentence for trying to smuggle an illegal immigrant into the United States. He was born in Peru but grew up in New York and Florida and became a U.S. citizen. While stationed with the Marines in San Diego in 2000, a friend dared him to try to sneak a young Peruvian guy across the border in the trunk of his car. Frank was caught and convicted, and at nineteen, he was thrown into La Mesa. Now he spends his days with Mother Antonia, helping her attend to the inmates who come in a steady stream to her door, at all hours, asking for everything from prescription medicines to advice on how to deal with their spouses.

Mother Antonia asks Frank about a female inmate. She's thirty-eight, dying of cancer, and has eight months left on a six-year sentence for a minor drug conviction. Mother Antonia is trying to persuade a judge to order her release on humanitarian grounds. Meanwhile, Mother Antonia's bringing medicine for the woman from the pharmacy to ease her pain. Frank says he's just been to visit her in the infirmary, which is clearly not his favorite place. All those sick people with every sort of disease, he says, shaking his head. He still can't believe that Mother Antonia touches them, even greets them with the traditional

Mexican kiss on the cheek. "These people have tuberculosis and stuff," he says to her, "and you just touch them — you even kiss them. I'm afraid to do that."

She has given Frank many of her favorite books, including *Once There Was a War*, John Steinbeck's dispatches of World War II. He never liked to read books before but now says he sees what he was missing. He wants to become a dentist when he gets out, his interest piqued by watching — and sometimes assisting — the dentists Mother Antonia brings to the prison to fix prisoners' teeth.

Mother Antonia unlocks the door to her *carraca,* as many prison cells are known, and leads us inside. She is home. "When I grew up in Beverly Hills, my father told me I'd brag all my life about where I lived," she says, looking around her cell and laughing out loud. "He was right!"

Her cell is concrete and cold. Her small bed is along the back wall, and two thin windows near the ceiling look out on a guard tower and barbed wire outside. A large crucifix hangs on one wall, and a few photos are scattered about on a small table, next to a Bible and a Spanish dictionary. Her pressed white blouses hang above a plastic garbage bag filled with hotel soaps and shampoos, stamped with "Hotel Del Coronado" or "Grand Hyatt," donations from friends in California that she passes out to inmates. She keeps a big jar of peanut butter near her bed so she always has something to give to any hungry prisoner. The door to the bathroom, nothing more than a bare toilet and a cold-water shower, is only a sheet. An oxygen tank sits next to her bed, evidence of her increasingly poor health.

She was born with an unusual problem with the tendons in her hand, which left her unable to make a fist. She underwent surgery to repair the problem when she was a child, the first of her long list of operations. Her real pain and health troubles began when she was nineteen and she lost her first child during delivery. Seven more pregnancies compounded the problems, and she developed a hiatal hernia. During an operation to repair that in 1992, when she was sixty-five, her esophagus was punctured by mistake. Over the next seven months she had six major operations, and during one of them, surgeons removed her spleen. For two years she could swallow only liquids. Friends jokingly called her the Sword Swallower because of the rubber tube she had to slide into her esophagus to keep it from closing up.

Her heart is weakening. She has two leaky valves and significant blockage in her arteries that give her trouble breathing. Doctors recommended that she leave the prison for health reasons. When she refused, they insisted that she keep an oxygen tank at her bedside. She sees it as part of her work, insisting that "my pains make me even more aware of other people's pain."

Mother Antonia has a million little sayings, distillations of what she has learned from seeing so much hardship and loss. She sprinkles them into her conversations constantly, like the little drops of chile sauce Mexicans put on everything from eggs to pizza.

"Life is a boomerang — what you do for others comes back to you."

"Everything you do either adds to the beauty of the world or takes away from it."

"Life is not a series of green lights."

Over the years, inmates have sometimes lied to her, stolen from her, even swiped her cell phone, but she doesn't let it get her down. She sums up her philosophy this way: "Live within the day. Forget about yesterday; it's over. Take everything bad and negative, and toss it away. Learn to step out from what is holding you back. To hate people will not change anything; to love them will."

Her mission has expanded over the years to include as many of Tijuana's poor and sick as she can reach. She even visits the dead. At the city morgue, bodies not claimed after nine days are buried in an unmarked common grave at the municipal cemetery. Mother Antonia often holds funerals for these people, who are sometimes known by only a number. Once a month, she holds a mass for all the unknown dead in Tijuana. The city supplies simple pine coffins, and she buys plots in the cemetery and small grave markers. On and off over the years, when there was no other transportation available, she would sometimes stand on the busy street outside the morgue and flag down a passing van or pickup truck to get a coffin to the cemetery.

"Excuse me, could you please help me for a minute?" she would ask, and soon a truck driver who happened to be passing by would be on his way to the cemetery with a nun and a coffin.

"She'll ask anyone to do anything," says Joanie Kenesie, her longtime friend and assistant. "And they always help her."

At the cemetery, she buys a cross to mark the grave and writes "We love you"

31

on it in Spanish. Then she calls over the grave diggers, vendors selling the crosses, anybody she can find to join in a prayer for a stranger as the coffin is lowered into the ground.

She helps people nobody else goes near. "Without her, we would have nothing," a seventy-year-old woman named Eloísa tells us. She lost both legs below the knee to leprosy. When Mother Antonia met Eloísa, her husband, Roberto, also a leper, was carrying her around the prison yard on his back. She had no other way to get around. Roberto had been arrested for selling drugs, because, he says, nobody would give a leper a job. Lost without him, Eloísa went out and sold drugs on the street as openly as possible, so she would be arrested and sent to La Mesa to be with him. While they were in prison, Mother Antonia brought them food and kept them company when nobody else would have anything to do with them. She paid to fix Eloísa's teeth, because, she tells us, "If you don't have legs, you should at least have a beautiful smile."

When they were released in 2003, Mother Antonia worked the phones until she found someone who was willing to rent to them. She asked a former inmate, whose freedom she had won by paying his bail, to paint the apartment for them, and she bought Eloísa a wheelchair.

As Mother Antonia's work became better known over the years, Mother Teresa visited with her on several trips to Tijuana and California. President Ronald Reagan wrote her a letter from the White House in 1982 praising her "devotion to a calling beyond the ordinary." Mexican President Vicente Fox has lauded her, and she was featured on a calendar honoring women who have made great contributions to Mexico.

She met Pope John Paul II in 1990 when he came to Chihuahua City to say Mass for hundreds of thousands of people. Bishop Emilio Berlie, then the bishop of Tijuana, chose Mother Antonia to carry the offertory gifts to the Pope. Over the microphone, the announcer called out Mother Antonia's name and said she was devoting her life to prisoners. She climbed the stairs to the platform where the Pope sat, and she knelt before him.

"Please pray for my prisoners," she asked.

He touched her cheek and handed her a rosary he had blessed.

She thanked him, then climbed down

from the stage, elated. Hers had always been an unorthodox mission, and it had been tough to persuade the official church to accept a twice-divorced mother as a Catholic sister. But there she was, being blessed by the Pope himself.

As she made her way through the massive crowd a man ran up to her, calling her name.

"Remember me?" he said. "You paid my fine to get me out of jail and brought me to the bus station. Thank you. Thank you."

She gave him the rosary the Pope had just handed to her.

"He ran through a million people to find me," she says. "It was meant to be his."

It is impossible to give Mother Antonia a gift, because she invariably gives it to someone else. Give her flowers, and they end up brightening a cancer ward. Give her candy, and prisoners end up eating it. She can always think of someone who needs it more than she does.

Mother Antonia is a nonstop coffee drinker who requires only a few hours of sleep a night. Every encounter with people seems to energize her even more, and we see that happen over and over.

On one typical day we spend with her, she wakes at five a.m. and tunes in to the news on the radio to "see who else I need to pray for today." She showers with cold water, then irons her veil on a small fold-up ironing board in her cell. Next she goes to the chapel to pray, and then to the *Grito,* the morning roll call of new prisoners. After that, she spends the next few hours in the prison, talking to inmates.

At ten o'clock, Joanie, who has been assisting Mother Antonia full-time since her husband died in 1997, drives her the two blocks to Casa Campos de San Miguel, the shelter she runs for poor women, where Mother Antonia keeps a small office. Out back are several dormitory-style rooms for women who have just been released from La Mesa, along with those who have come to visit an inmate and women who are suffering from cancer.

Gabriela García Loeza is waiting for Mother Antonia outside Casa Campos as we arrive, her eyes swollen from crying. She was discharged from prison the night before and has been up all night. She tells Mother Antonia she has no money to go anywhere.

Mother Antonia hugs her and tells her she is going to give her a bus ticket to Mexico City, where Gabriela has family. In the meantime, she should stay here.

Gabriela calms down and comes into the house, heading to the kitchen, where some of the sisters who have joined Mother Antonia's unusual religious community cook her lunch.

We follow Mother Antonia into her office, and before she can sit down to tackle her stack of phone messages, the wife of a La Mesa guard arrives, frantic: "My husband said you help everybody. Can you help him? He's a good man, but now he is changed. I think he's using drugs. He is very aggressive. He doesn't eat. He doesn't sleep. Please, please, what are we going to do?"

Mother Antonia listens from behind her desk, where she keeps miniature Mexican, U.S., and Irish flags. She pulls out her dog-eared book of telephone numbers and is soon talking to the state's director of public security. She asks him: If a guard voluntarily acknowledged that he had a drug or alcohol addiction and wanted to take time off to go into rehab, would he promise her that the man wouldn't be fired?

Sure, he says.

"You promise me, right?"

They talk about the need to start an Alcoholics Anonymous program for the guards. When the call ends, Mother Antonia turns to the wife and urges her to help her husband rather than criticize him. Then she asks for his cell number and dials it.

"Víctor! This is Madre Antonia. I need you to come to my cell Saturday. I need your help with something."

"Thank you! Thank you!" the wife cries out, comforted that Mother Antonia will talk to him. She leaves, walking past the pile of Winnie the Poohs and stuffed animals that a donor from California has dropped off in the living room. By mid-afternoon, fifty children have come to the door and left with a new toy.

There are also restaurant-size cans of crushed pineapple and bags of used designer clothing; Nine West black sandals sit atop one pile. Everything goes to the prisoners, their families, and the needy of Tijuana. Literally tons of it every month. While we are there, a man drops off sixty liters of donated milk and juice.

A little girl pads around the living room. She had ended up in an orphanage because her mother, who was suffering from schizophrenia, couldn't care for her. One of the sisters in Mother Antonia's community adopted her, and now the little girl lives here, too.

The doorbell rings every few minutes. A man asks for a clean shirt. A boy asks for a pair of shoes. A twenty-year-old man asks for money to see a dentist; he has no upper teeth. The sisters find the shirt and shoes, and Mother Antonia writes a note to a dentist asking him to fix the man's teeth; she'll pay, as always.

Just as we are leaving, a man pulls up in an old beige Mustang. His name is Adam, and he is thirty-three. He tells Mother Antonia that he wants to kill himself, and that some instinct told him to come find her.

She puts her arms around him and hugs him.

"That is what I needed," he says.

The other sisters take him inside to chat for the afternoon and to fill him with warm food.

Mother Antonia then takes us with her across the border in her old blue Mazda, which was a donation, to get some papers notarized in San Ysidro, near San Diego. As she waits in line at the crowded crossing, a Mexican border guard recognizes her and walks up.

"Hi, Mama!" he says. "Can I please ask you a favor? Can you pray for my mother? She's sick."

Mother Antonia asks her name and promises to pray for her.

At the notary's office, a clerk, about fifty years old, comes up to her and whispers.

"Madre Antonia," he says. "I'm one of your sons. I was in La Mesa fourteen years ago."

He is fighting back tears. Mother Antonia touches him gently and says she is happy to see him doing so well.

Back at La Mesa, she checks with the guards at the Rooster House. The smell inside had been so overpowering in the morning that she asked that they clean it out, which they have.

A man is waiting for her near her cell. He says his catheter has been emptying urine into the same plastic bag for too long and asks if she can please get him a new one. She makes a note to take care of it before the day is out.

She is feeling a little tired, and she knows that her day — like all her days — won't end until late at night. There will be a steady stream of inmates coming to her door with every kind of problem. She lies down for a few minutes, twists the valve on her oxygen tank, puts the mask over her face, and allows herself a few long, deep breaths.

"People say what I'm doing is such a great sacrifice, but it is not," she says, now feeling a little stronger. "I don't think of it as sacrifice. It's only a sacrifice when you do something you don't want to."

Mother Antonia has not come to this point easily. She speaks about her divorces with obvious pain, and she remembers late nights of doubting herself sitting alone after her kids were asleep, and wondering what lay ahead for her and for them. She knows she made lots of mistakes. She married too young the first time, too impulsively the second.

"It hasn't always been easy for her," says her oldest daughter, Kathleen, a family and marriage counselor in San Diego. "She went through so many trials, but they made her who she is. Her empathy and compassion have grown so much through her own suffering. She has struggled to get to this happiness."

TWO

HOLLYWOOD GIRL

Mother Antonia was born in Los Angeles on the first of December 1926 and christened Mary Clarke. No middle name. Her first-generation Irish-American parents valued simplicity. The golden-haired baby would be Mary, nothing more, nothing showier, a name freighted with faith that Irish Catholics have bestowed upon their children by the millions as an act of honor and hope.

Her father, Joseph Clarke, grew up in New York at the beginning of the twentieth century, the son of a fisherman who drowned at sea before his first birthday and a mother who scrubbed floors and washed clothes for people who could afford not to. Joseph missed many weeks of school over the years helping his mother earn money, but the understanding nuns at the parish school awarded him a diploma that said he had completed the eighth grade.

What he lacked in advantages, he made up for with personality and engaging goodness, and these qualities lifted his fortunes as a young man. At seventeen, Joseph applied to a big firm in New Jersey for a job selling carbon paper and typewriter ribbons, the hottest technology in American offices. Charming and persuasive, with dark good looks and hazel eyes, he came across as unusually confident without any trace of egotism. Though he had no experience, he was sure he could knock on any door and come away with a sale. "Being hungry," he often said, "makes you succeed."

He didn't have an appropriate suit for an interview, so he assembled the best of his poor boy's clothing and marched into the company president's office. When the man told him to sit down and take off his coat, Joseph answered that he could not because his pants were torn. His directness and humility impressed the president, who peeled some bills from a money roll in his pocket and told Joseph to buy himself a suit so he'd look sharp on his sales calls. "Mr. Clarke," the boss said, "I think you are one guy who can sell."

A year later, the young man married Kathleen Mary Reilly, also the child of Irish immigrants and seven years his senior. They shared a love of words — his gift was speaking, hers was writing. They moved together to Los Angeles when Joseph became the West Coast salesman for Peerless Imperial Manufacturing Co. of New Jersey.

A son, Joseph Jr., arrived soon afterward, followed by two daughters, Mary and Kathleen. Then in April 1929, before Mary turned three, her mother began bleeding internally during the early stages of a fourth pregnancy. Her doctor proposed surgery, which could save her life at the expense of the baby's, but she refused because of her deeply held religious beliefs. The doctor told her she would die if they didn't operate. "Well, then I'll be dead," Kathleen snapped back, "but it will be God's will." When he protested, she picked up a book from her bedside and threw it at him. Two days later she and her unborn baby were dead.

In the brutal economy of the Great Depression, the grieving Joseph lost his job. Unemployed, a widower at twenty-four, his finances were so precarious he had to borrow money to bury his wife. But he was accustomed to loss and poverty and steeled himself to face hardship. Joseph Clarke carried his family through the twin crises with a peaceful inner strength that Mary would later learn she had inherited.

Joseph picked up odd jobs, any job, to feed his family. He was a single father who showered his children with love and attention. Mary vividly recalls how he would sit by her bedside and sing her to sleep with Irish ballads, like "The Rose of Tralee":

*She was
lovely and fair
as the rose of the summer
yet 'twas not her beauty
alone that won me
Oh, no! 'twas the truth
in her eye ever dawning
that made me love Mary,
the Rose of Tralee.*

Two years after Kathleen died, Joseph married Marion Hadley, a widow with a teenage son named Bill. The family's fortunes soon rebounded when Joseph's old company hired him back as World War II escalated, and they would never falter again. Business boomed as defense contractors ordered huge volumes of his supplies. Movie studios consumed crates of carbon paper keeping tabs on a record output of movies and the contracts of their stables of stars. In 1942, the Clarkes moved to a lavish house on Tower Road in Beverly Hills, where their celebrity neighbors included William Powell, Hedy Lamarr, John Barrymore, and Dinah Shore. Joseph, who had skipped school as a boy to earn a few bucks caddying for wealthy golfers, joined the Riviera Country Club and regularly took the family to dine in the fanciest restaurants on La Cienega Boulevard. As his fortunes rose, he bought them an eleven-bedroom, eleven-bathroom summer home on a hill in Laguna Beach, overlooking the ocean.

Wealth never blinded him to the needs of the poor, however, and his children learned from his example. Whenever someone approached him on the street selling apples or pencils, he always bought and never haggled over the price. He walked up the steep Temple Street hill in Los Angeles instead of taking the streetcar, and he explained to the kids that the nickel he saved was going to the Maryknoll Missionaries, his favorite charity. A visiting Maryknoll priest once told Mary about a child with leprosy who played the piano with her knuckles. The image seized Mary's imagination, and she daydreamed about someday becoming a missionary herself.

Joseph rarely missed a chance to teach a lesson, often taught when he took his children with him on business trips. On a trip to Chicago, five-year-old Mary met a young couple staying on the same floor of their hotel. They invited the girl into their room for a cookie. When they weren't looking, Mary swiped a nickel off a table; later she offered it to her stepmother, saying she should buy herself a pair of stockings.

"Where did you get that?" her stepmother asked.

"A nice lady gave it to me," she replied, but Marion wasn't buying it.

When her father returned, he quickly got to the truth and erupted in a flowing Celtic rage: "So those nice people invite you in and you repay them by taking their money? You are going to go down the hall and give it back to them. Knock on the door, and when they answer tell them, 'I am the thief who stole this nickel.'" Mary made the grim walk like a condemned criminal and gave back the nickel, barely able to speak from the humiliation.

Joseph took Mary on another business trip to Pennsylvania, where they visited a coal mine. She saw the harsh conditions and listened as her father complained that the little guys suffer while the rich grow richer off their sweat. Miners made a few dollars a week, he said, while the owners "walk on mink rugs." Joseph warned her never to cross a picket line and always to take the side of workers demanding fair wages and decent conditions.

Some of Joseph's favorite colleagues and customers were Jewish men; the closest of these friends was Fred Rothman, whom the Clarke kids called "Uncle Fred." As the Nazis came to power in Germany, Joseph perceived earlier than most Americans the grave peril facing European Jews. Dinner table conversations among Joseph and his friends were filled with frustration at the governments in Washington and Europe that did nothing in the face of the growing persecution. Mary, in her early teens, listened as the men discussed plans to send money through a network of contacts to help people escape. Joseph saved at least one man, whom Mary knew as Mr. Gurtz, from the Nazis by paying his way to Los Angeles and getting him a job.

Later, as the horrifying reality of the concentration camps came into focus, the dinner conversation among Joseph and his friends turned to the evil of indifference and inaction, ideas that deeply affected

Mary. She found it hard to understand how families all around the world could go happily about their lives as the horror escalated. She developed a deep empathy for the Jews and respect for their faith that she would later incorporate into her mission. The cross Mother Antonia wears around her neck today is fashioned from nails and copper wire by La Mesa inmates, and at its center is a large Star of David.

Mary was always more serious than she appeared. As she grew, she became increasingly preoccupied by the suffering of people beyond her comfortable world, from the soldiers in Europe to the hungry children of China. She read, over and over, John Steinbeck's *In Dubious Battle*, about the conditions of migrant workers in California, as well as Jan Valtin's *Out of the Night*, which documented the crushing of the working class in Fascist Germany. The topic of social justice didn't interest most of her friends. So on many afternoons, she would tuck a book under her arm and clamber down the rocks to read in a cave she discovered at Laguna Beach. This was her escape world, she thought, and there, with the waves crashing against the rocks and just enough light slanting in, she read in solitude, escaping not from, but into, the troubles of the world.

Mary turned fifteen just before Pearl Harbor. Within ten days of her birthday, America was at war and her stepbrother, Bill, was dead in a military plane crash. Mary's older brother, Joseph, immediately enlisted in the Navy and was soon stationed aboard a minesweeper in the Pacific and writing letters home describing terrible fighting in the Solomon Islands.

The war came to dominate every aspect of her life. Mary talked recruiters into letting her join the Women's Ambulance Corps, an auxiliary force created to help military and civilian doctors in case of an attack, even though the minimum age was eighteen. Walking door to door in her fancy neighborhood, she collected items for a benefit auction to aid soldiers. One day she worked up the courage to knock on the door of the famous singer Eddie Cantor. She could hear him practicing upstairs, but when he heard her at the door he came flying down the stairs. "What's this about ten dollars for my autograph?" he teased her. "What kind of a split am I going to get?"

The Clarkes' beautiful beach house in Laguna was south of Los Angeles, near the El Toro military base, where thousands of men shipped out to war. Mary's father often invited Marines and their wives to use the house for their last good-byes. Mary's own high school friends soon joined the tide of young men headed to war. The student body president left full of promise and returned minus a leg, amputated, so they said, on the battlefield.

Everything about Mary's teenage years was intense. Families huddled around radios for the latest news from the battlefields and lived in fear of telegrams bearing devastating news. Couples rushed off to town halls to get married before the men shipped out. But each place in America filtered the war through its own culture, and Hollywood's filter was, as ever, glamour. Bob Hope wisecracked for the troops; Betty Grable posed for pinup calendars. This, too, was Mary Clarke's life. She was a wealthy girl who wore stylish dresses to parties and sipped from demitasse cups. She was growing into a head-turning beauty, and when she tagged along with her father to call on his customers, she easily sweet-talked studio guards into letting her behind the scenes of Hollywood's golden age. Her teenage crush on Cary Grant was nearly suffocating; she memorized long passages from *Gunga Din* and

other films of his during sigh-filled afternoons at the Pantages Theater in Hollywood.

On a trip to New York, she had dinner
with the famed Hollywood choreographer
Busby Berkeley in a trendy restaurant
called The Epicure, along with a friend
who was a model and had already landed
on a magazine cover. Berkeley, who had
made Esther Williams into a swimsuit su-
perstar, gushed over Mary, and after they
bantered for a bit, he said she should be in
pictures. "You are the one I want," he told
her. "You are something special." But
Mary had seen too many movie stars up
close to be easily seduced by celebrity. She
knew what she wanted from life, and that
wasn't it.

What Mary desperately, impatiently,
wanted was to marry and have children.
She had a certain kind of man in mind.
She knew about money, and she thought it
was overrated. Her father's wealthy friends
spent sixty or eighty hours a week at the
office, then spent evenings working the
telephone. To her way of thinking, it would
be better to marry a tradesman with grease
on his hands, a guy who came home at five
o'clock, washed up in the kitchen sink, and
left his work right there in the lather.

But the war took its toll on one promising relationship after another. The first boy she kissed was Billy Shardlo, an eighteen-year-old Russian Jew, nephew of Uncle Fred Rothman. Billy joined the Marines and died charging onto the beach at Guadalcanal. Andres was a young man she dated for several months before he left for Army flight school. During his brief return to a base near Hollywood, she went to visit him in high heels, a pretty dress, a hat, and gloves. "Tell the lieutenant his wife is here," the guard called out when she reached the gate. It thrilled her to be called somebody's wife. Andres shipped out to the Pacific and never came back.

Next she met Edward Thomas Connor, a bright and thoughtful nineteen-year-old from Pennsylvania. Eddie fell hard for Mary, and she was enchanted by him, but they had time for only a few dates before he headed to the South Pacific. They wrote often and passionately and even brought up marriage, but Mary knew Eddie wanted to finish college before settling down, and she didn't want to wait that long to be a bride.

On a spring day in 1945, when she was eighteen, Mary went to Seattle with her family. Her brother's minesweeper was due for a port call, and Mary stood with hundreds of other families and girlfriends as the sailors came down the gangway. She spotted Joseph amid all the sailors in their blue uniforms, but it was his buddy, Ray Monahan, who caught her eye. As she listened to their stories of war, Mary was immediately taken by Ray; he was exactly the kind of handsome, strong-bodied man she had been dreaming of. They spent a few days together in Seattle before he shipped out again. The war ended that summer, and he came back alive.

When he visited Mary in Beverly Hills, Ray recited poetry from memory, and he made her laugh. They spent long happy evenings singing together, Ray at the piano, a cigarette hanging from the corner of his mouth, and Mary with her arm draped around his neck. Their courtship was short and passionate, and they married in early 1946, with a church ceremony and an elegant reception at the Beverly Hills Hotel. She was nineteen and he not quite twenty-one.

Mary loved the way her new name, Mary Monahan, rang in her ears. She adored being a wife, and she and Ray were eager to be parents. After a month of marriage, and not instantly pregnant, she took out her impatience on the Virgin Mary, shaking the little statue on her dresser and shouting, "You know that I want to have a baby!"

Pregnancy came soon enough, plagued by sickness and punctuated by grief. Mary struggled through a fifty-seven-hour labor and finally gave birth to a baby boy whose brain had been crushed by the efforts to deliver him. A nurse brought the baby to Mary, who was barely strong enough to hold him. That was the only time she held her son, named Joseph after her father; the child died three days later. Mary's injuries from that birth would cause her pain for the rest of her life.

The doctors advised Mary to stay in the hospital, but the sound of babies crying was too much for her. Ray carried her up the stairs of her parents' house and settled her into bed. "I'm so sorry," he said, "but I'm so happy you are alive."

After the loss, Mary began going to church daily and, painful though it was, found that the tragedy strengthened her faith. She believed that somehow, in some form, her baby would never leave her. A thoughtful priest told her that now she had a little saint in heaven, and that she would have to struggle all her life to join him.

"When Joseph died, my church was once again there to lift me up," she says. She found herself praying to her child, "Help me, Joseph. Help me, Joseph." Almost sixty years later, she still prays to him and asks him to watch over his brothers and sisters and others in need.

"I do understand why some people say, 'How could God do this to me?' " she says. "But that did not happen to me. I never thought Joseph's death had anything to do with punishment." She even prayed for the doctor who should have performed a cesarean section and saved Joseph's life. "He cried when Joseph died," she recalls, "and I knew how terrible he must have felt when he realized he could have saved the baby."

Ray reacted differently to the loss. He poured himself into his job as a newspaper distributor and seemed to want to succeed too fast. Mary worried that he might be trying to emulate her father, who had lent him the money to get started. Ray started gambling with cash he was taking in at work. He started coming home later and later, and his debts piled up. Mary didn't mind having little money, but she did mind owing people, and she couldn't face the milkman when she didn't have enough money to pay him. The gravity of her marriage vows began to feel like a dead weight. Such a short time ago she had been a daydreaming teenager, and now she was an adult with problems she had never imagined.

"I'm weak when I fall in love," she says. "I walk on air. I lose my appetite. I can't think straight. I'm not one to be sensible. My heart has always been my guide. I think you could say my heart drove me to do the best things in my life, and also to make my most serious mistakes."

She and Ray spent less and less time together. They no longer prayed together in the morning or played board games at night. In the pews of St. Anne's Church, across the street from their apartment, she felt closer to her church than ever before, but at the same time she felt she was failing it. Marriage vows were sacred, but she wasn't sure she could keep hers. She graded herself on a mental report card: an A for "in sickness and in health," a C for "richer or poorer" — but an F in "for better or for worse."

Though Mary cherished her church, she was increasingly struggling with many of its rules and teachings. After Joseph died, one teaching in particular tore at her: that the souls of unbaptized babies were barred from Heaven and banished to Limbo. She never believed in Limbo, and she refused to accept that God would keep innocent babies out of Heaven. Limbo later faded from church teaching, but in those days, the church taught that it was as real as fish on Friday.

Her mother had a faith so rock-solid that she had chosen to die rather than risk violating its teaching, but Mary was certain that "God is more forgiving than church rules." So she tried to think less about the Shalts and Shalt Nots and focused on the big picture: God loves and forgives everyone. Every person matters. People have an obligation to help the needy.

Truth be told, she had never gone strictly by the book. Mary had always sought out and cherished mentors who nurtured freedom of thought. At school, she was inspired by Sister Claire Madeleine, a blur of energy and brains in a stiff white wimple and full black habit. Sister Claire loved the church, but she wasn't afraid to point out its shortcomings to her students. She acknowledged the sinful lapses of Renaissance popes and railed against injustices done to American blacks. Sister Claire preached social justice and admired those who defeated oppression and bigotry by sheer integrity. She quoted Booker T.

Washington, saying, "I let no man drag me down so low as to make me hate him."

As Mary struggled with her grief and guilt, she remembered Sister Claire. One incident seemed to capture the quality of grace and forgiveness that she represented. When Mary was in school, she received a letter from her brother. Joseph loved Mexico. His Spanish was good enough that he sometimes worked as a translator in the Navy. In his letter, he asked Mary to go to a Mexican church in Los Angeles on December 12, the feast day of Our Lady of Guadalupe. He asked that she lay flowers in honor of Mexico's patron saint.

Mary proudly showed the letter to the nuns at her school, and one after another had the same quibble: "He spelled Communion wrong." Joseph had written the word the Spanish way, with a single "m." As though it mattered. Only Sister Claire gushed about the beauty of the letter — and of the spirit behind it — and Mary admired her focus on the good in things, rather than an endless search for flaws.

Her stepmother, Marion, encouraged Mary's freedom of conscience. At St. Monica's, the Catholic high school Mary attended in Los Angeles, an assistant principal once summoned the girl and her stepmother to the office to discuss an "issue of morals." Marion Hadley was more amused than upset at being called in. Having been raised an Episcopalian, she was a Catholic by choice, not from the cradle, and she was not afraid to dissent in matters she considered minor. She knew well that her daughter frequently tested limits, but she also knew the girl had no trouble whatsoever with her morals. As they drove to the school, she told Mary, "Remember, I'm on your side."

Mary wondered which of the school's many rules she had been caught breaking. Had someone seen her smoking a cigarette? Had she been seen alone with a boy? Had she been spotted in a restaurant that served alcohol? She asked the nun who ushered them into the meeting, "This is about something that is immoral in what sense? Something you have decided is immoral? Is it something I should go to confession for?" Her confident questioning took the sister aback, and she responded, "You know, Mary, you should be a lawyer."

It turned out a mother had complained that Mary had pointed to her daughter's plump belly and ordered, "Pull in Junior," an expression at the time that simply meant to suck in your gut. But even joking about an unmarried girl being pregnant was a serious offense to that unsmiling nun.

Now, living with Ray, beset by grief, and plagued by doubts, Mary scraped her faith to its foundation. She asked God why life was so harsh, full of pain, and unfair to so many people. One morning she read in the paper about a boy in a correctional school who had been beaten to death for talking in the dining room. Unable to clear her mind of that image, she took a long bus ride to the school and stood outside to say a rosary. She had to do something.

Many mornings, she was often the only person in the pews for Mass at St. Anne's, a Melkite Catholic church — which belongs to the Eastern Rite, rather than the Latin Rite. The split between East and West went back a thousand years, but it meant little to Mary. True, she had been baptized and married in the Latin Rite, and yes, there were differences between the churches. Although Eastern and Latin Rite churches agreed on the substance of Catholic teaching, their rituals and laws brooked many differences. Eastern Rite priests were allowed to wed, for example. These distinctions mattered greatly to church officials, but Mary preferred to see what the two rites shared. She believed a

Catholic sacrament was the same whether it was performed in Arabic or Latin or English. For that matter, she felt sure that God approved of all good works and prayer, whether they came from a church, a mosque, or a synagogue.

Mary grew close to the St. Anne's parish priest, Monsignor Clement Salman. When she became pregnant again shortly after her first baby's death, she sometimes felt too sick to cross the street. So Salman climbed the stairs to her apartment and administered Communion there. As the arrival of Mary's baby drew near, it seemed only natural to silently promise St. Anne that she would baptize the baby in her church.

She was determined to keep that promise when her second child, James Patrick Monahan, was born. But Salman told her she needed permission from church officials. So she called the priest at the nearest Latin Rite church, who answered abruptly that he wouldn't permit the sacraments to be performed at St. Anne's.

Then he hung up on her.

Salman pleaded with her not to pursue the matter. He told her that the bishop's office had called and accused him of trying to lure parishioners from other churches — "sheep stealing," as priests called it. But she was undeterred. She called Bishop Timothy Manning, who later became a cardinal, to plead her case.

"Your name is Monahan, and you are Irish," said the puzzled bishop. Why wouldn't she want her child baptized in the church of her heritage? Mary argued that a sacrament is a sacrament.

Finally, after much back and forth, Mary told him, "But I made a promise to St. Anne. Doesn't a promise mean anything?"

"A promise to St. Anne?" Manning answered. "Nobody told me you made a promise to St. Anne." Within the hour, Salman came chugging up her stairs with the news that Bishop Manning had called to say that he could baptize her baby. Mary found it deeply satisfying that what she saw as the small-minded attitude of a local priest had been overruled.

A new, healthy baby failed to bring Ray closer to her, though. Her husband's gambling persisted, while his career languished. Mary convinced him they should move to Denver, where his parents lived, away from his gambling buddies. There he set up a business running vending machines, but before long, he fell behind on payments to his suppliers and the business failed. Ray then found work in newspaper distribution, but he was bored by it, and Mary worried about the family's financial security. Less than a year after she gave birth to Jimmy, she was pregnant again with her first daughter, Kathleen. In 1949, with two kids to care for, Mary was frustrated and disillusioned.

When Ray came home one day, angry at someone at work, and threatened to quit his job, she was furious.

"You're gonna quit?" she snapped at him. "How can you quit? You've got kids! You've got me!"

Their problems mounted, but Ray never even acknowledged the situation. Mary was stunned when he suggested one day that the answer to their problems was another baby. She had given birth three times in three years. She felt physically exhausted. For better had become for worse, and despite her marriage vows, she realized that she just didn't love him anymore.

"There sometimes comes a time in marriage when feelings change," she says now. "Something happens, and you never feel the same again. Love stops sometimes."

She told herself it would be a temporary separation.

Mary went home to California with her two children. Her father set her up in a little apartment, and she began working to support her one-parent family. One job wasn't enough, so she found two. Now and then, Ray would call from Denver to tell her that he wanted them all to be together, and her response was always the same: Send us the tickets and we will come home. In her mind, the tickets became a measure of his responsibility and commitment.

They never arrived.

Ray took the kids to Denver for a visit once. By then, he had become a police officer. The visit was nearly a disaster: Jimmy got his hands on his father's gun and fired a shot through a door. After only a few days, Ray brought the kids back to Los Angeles, where they had one sad, final meeting in the airport.

"They don't even know who I am," Ray said.

Mary took his hands in hers and said good-bye. On the drive home, she willed her eyes to stay dry so the kids wouldn't see her crying.

At twenty-four, Mary felt like a coward and a failure, doomed to be divorced from her husband and separated from her church. But she was determined to make a better life for her and her children, and she threw herself into a new routine as a working mother.

THREE

SALESMAN FOR THE POOR

Mary worked part-time for her father's company and part-time in a real estate office he owned in Bel-Air, but her hardest work was at home. She hired someone to help with Jim and Kathleen, which turned out to be traumatic. They hated her leaving in the morning, and she cried on her way out the door when they looked at her and asked, "Going to *wohk* today?"

"It was terrible," she says. "I have never stopped feeling it to this day; every time I see a woman who is trying to work and raise kids, I feel for her. If they have baby-sitters from the time they're very little, it's different. But I had always been home with them." There was no way around working. She couldn't live on her father's largesse forever, and she needed to bring some cash into the house. She left the house early every morning but always tried to be home by five to spend time with the kids.

As hard as it was, Mary also felt sure she was doing the right thing. She needed to start a new life. There would be new disappointments, she was sure, but for the moment she was just twenty-four and feeling more alive than she had in years. She was also discovering that she was good at work. She had gotten to know her father's business growing up, and now she was finding that the real estate office in particular was a place where she could thrive.

Over the next few months, she also started getting back into the Hollywood social scene, often in the company of her stylish and wealthy girlfriend Grace Anderson. She didn't want her failed marriage to be her last. She and Grace drew lots of attention from the boys, and Mary was determined to find someone new in her life. Her yardstick had changed in one significant way, though; he didn't simply have to want kids, he had to be crazy about hers. "Ask any single mother," she says. "The first quality you look for in a man is, 'How do they feel about my children?' "

Mary and Grace went to a golf tournament in Palm Springs, where Grace's family had rented out the estate of the Duncan family, who had earned a fortune selling yo-yos. Around the clubhouse the men were fawning over Grace and Mary — including Carl Brenner, a tall and athletic man Mary had met a couple of years before at her sister's wedding. Carl had come to the wedding with several of his football player friends; Ray had thought they were a bunch of dumb lunks and had cracked that "the biggest muscle they have is between their ears." She hadn't taken much notice of Carl then, but he started calling her after the meeting at Palm Springs, and she was thrilled. Impulsively — too impulsively, she now realizes — she and Carl started seeing each other.

Carl was a powerful presence, an ash-blond University of Southern California grad with a huge personality and enormous physical gifts. He stood six foot two and dressed in Brooks Brothers suits and Florsheim shoes, never rich but always looking it, a handsome man's man, a tough guy with a rock for a chin. Not only a talented golfer, he was a competitive swimmer and had played baseball well enough to attract scouts from the New York Yankees. Later he earned a pilot's license for fun and taught others to fly, too. Mary found his competitive spirit and his energy for life extremely seductive, and, more important, she loved how he carried her children as easily as a couple of footballs. "That's the biggest gift he could have given me," she says. "He loved being with the kids." Mary was swept up in Carl's charm, and their relationship took off like a California brushfire.

As soon as her divorce papers were finalized, they were married on a romantic adventure to Las Vegas in 1950, "driving as fast as we could" to get there. Looking back, she realizes she rushed into her second marriage too soon. "I was too much in love, and too Catholic, to have a relationship that wasn't somehow binding," she says. "In those days, it was the decent thing to do. I once heard Bette Davis say that if she could have had the kinds of relationships that are allowed now, she wouldn't have been married five times. I believed that."

Almost from the beginning, Mary realized that her marriage to Carl was going to be more complicated than she had imagined. She craved a true partnership, and Carl quickly made it clear to Mary that he wanted a pretty wife who stayed out of his business. He didn't tell her how much money he made or who his friends were. He didn't even invite her to the country club where he golfed and spent much of his free time. Though he was a loving father to the children, he became emotionally distant and aloof with Mary.

"I was terribly in love with him, and every day I tried to make him happy with me and with his household," she says. "But then one day I realized there are some people for whom nothing in the world you do can make them happy. Nothing. I realized that Carl was in that category. He'd be the kind who would walk in, and you could have everything, flowers on the table and a cake in the oven, and a beautiful dress on, and he'd find something that was wrong. He just couldn't say, 'Everything's nice, everything's wonderful.' It just stuck in his throat."

Though the prospect of life with such a dissatisfying marriage was sobering, the pain and guilt of leaving Ray still stung her, and she was determined to find a way to make things work with Carl. She tried to focus on his good qualities: He didn't drink, he worked hard, and he loved the children. She thought to herself, "I'm going to love him for what he is, and have my own life." She loved being a mother, and she threw herself into raising her children.

Her first baby with Carl, Theresa, was born in 1952, followed by Carol in 1953 and Tom in 1955 — their last two, Elizabeth and Anthony, would come a bit later, in 1959 and 1961. She made them pancakes with Mickey Mouse ears and cakes shaped like bunnies and lambs on Easter, and dedicated herself to her home, cleaning and polishing, sometimes even using a toothbrush to clean the inside of her lampshades. Every Sunday, she took the kids to church, scrubbed little ducks all in a row, while Carl played golf with his friends.

She was not allowed to receive Communion because in the eyes of the Catholic Church, which does not recognize divorce, she was still married to Ray and living with a man who was not her husband. Still, she stayed close to the church and always attended Mass. Although she felt like a second-class citizen and knew others might gossip about why she never approached the Communion rail, she found she couldn't really fault the church for wanting to make marriage vows hard to break.

Even so, they were hard years for her because of her strained relations with the church and her troubles with Carl. They rarely fought, but the gulf between them was widening. She once found him packing a suitcase, and when she asked where he was going he said simply, "On vacation." She doubted he was going alone. Furious and hurt, she didn't walk out because she couldn't bear the thought of putting her children through the pain of divorce again.

They increasingly lived in two separate worlds. A working mother in the mid-1950s was an exception, but she excelled at it and she enjoyed the independence. She liked the thrill of dazzling movie executives and defense contractors accustomed to men pitching them deals, not a blonde in a knockout dress. And after her experience with Ray, she never again wanted to fully depend on her husband's income; she was protecting herself and her children, even though it was exhausting. The kids spent the day with a nanny or at school, and she returned home again by four or five to make dinner.

Mary was spending many late nights by herself, thinking about how things had turned out in her life. She would sit at the dining room table, often surrounded by a stack of bills, smoking cigarettes and trying to identify a gnawing feeling inside her, a sense that there were important things she needed to do. She felt like her life wasn't being used as it was meant to be. Work was fun and challenging, but it wasn't fulfilling.

She wanted to do something more meaningful than keeping offices well supplied or setting the perfect dinner table. Raising seven children was wonderful, but she began to feel she should be contributing somehow to something larger.

Her brother Joseph finally gave her the perfect idea. Now captain of a merchant ship in Asia, Joseph wrote to her about the terrible suffering he was seeing in Korea after the war. He had been working with missionaries to help bring donated clothes, food, and medicine to war orphans. His letters spoke admiringly of a Maryknoll named Sister Mary Angelica O'Leary, who had become his guide through the misery. She had asked him to drum up contributions from the United States, and Joseph came up with a plan. He asked Mary to go down to the docks near Los Angeles to find ships heading for Korea; if she could find a sympathetic captain, he knew she could persuade him to carry boxes of relief supplies. That gave Mary the opening she'd been looking for. She hustled down to the docks and started asking around. The captains not only agreed to help her, but they were delighted to ferry aid from the world's richest country to one of its most wounded. She felt a new sense of purpose and enthusiasm welling up inside her that she had not felt in years.

She began soliciting neighbors, friends, work contacts, companies — anybody who might have old clothes, shoes, medicine — anything. Filling her car with boxes, she drove down to the docks and then she went right back out to find more. She spent long hours on the phone after the kids went to bed, calling hospitals, medical supply companies, and friends to ask them for donations. When she took her own kids to the doctor, she always left with boxes of samples, vitamins, and medicines for her cause. The family garage in Granada Hills, a comfortable L.A. suburb, became a warehouse, stuffed to the ceiling with donations.

The kids loved the fun new energy that filled the house. Kathleen and Jim were now about seven and eight, and Carol and Theresa were about three and four — old enough to like playing around all the crazy boxes of stuff in the garage. Carl was less enthusiastic. He didn't exactly object, but he was cool about her charity work and hated the clutter and boxes overflowing from the garage, where he often couldn't find the space to park his car.

"Why don't you just move us out in the

street — then you can use the whole house," he would say to her.

Sometimes in the evenings Mary would remember that Carl was about to arrive, and she'd say to the kids and their neighborhood friends, "Daddy's coming home!" Everyone would scramble to stack up boxes as neatly as possible, so it would look a little better when Carl opened the garage door.

Despite the tension with Carl, Mary had never felt so good at anything in her life, or so fulfilled, knowing that ships were sailing for Korea carrying donations that she had put together. The satisfaction of landing a new account at work now seemed trivial compared with helping desperate children in Korea. People said to her, "If you ever applied this energy and this love you have for the poor to your business, you'd be a rich woman." But they didn't understand her.

Not long after Mary's loads of goods started arriving in Korea, Sister Angelica came to California for a visit. As they surveyed the boxes of donations in Mary's garage together, Mary said she had one box she didn't know what to do with, filled with unmatched single shoes. Sister Angelica told her to send the shoes anyway, because they would find a home. In Korea, she knew plenty of children with only one foot. Those words drove Mary even harder.

When her nephew, Danny, became ill with leukemia in 1954, Mary was introduced to City of Hope, the world-renowned hospital in Duarte, California. A long association with the hospital followed, providing her a way to do charitable works much closer to home and to spend time with those she was helping.

Danny, the only son of Mary's sister, Kathleen, had been sent to City of Hope after doctors said he had just a few months to live. Mary visited him regularly, and on the day before he died, he looked up at her and asked her about God.

"There is a heaven, isn't there, Aunt Mary?"

"Yes, there is."

"Is it the wonderful place that everybody says it is?"

"Yes, Danny, it is."

"Then why is everybody sad that I'm going there?"

Danny had watched other children in beds around him die, but rather than become afraid, he seemed sure he would be going on to an afterlife, even if the adults around him did not.

"You know, Aunt Mary, I don't mind going to heaven. But I wish my mother could come with me."

The next day he looked up at his mother and said, "Hold me, hold me. Hold me with both arms."

As she did, he looked at her blankly and said, "Mother, I can't see you anymore."

Then he closed his eyes and died.

The care Danny received at City of Hope inspired Mary. If you could not cure cancer, you certainly could help children and families through it. They treated every child like royalty, whether or not their families could pay. No matter how sick they were, no matter how much they were suffering, and whatever their background, the hospital welcomed them. Mary realized that the care she saw at City of Hope was a model for how she wanted to spend her life. The satisfaction she felt helping the poor on the other side of the world was fantastic, but she could directly care for the children at City of Hope. Sometimes at work in Beverly Hills she would suddenly find herself driving to the hospital, arriving with toys or candy. She had persuaded the See's Candy company to give her huge boxes of imperfectly shaped, but perfectly delicious, castoffs.

For several years she ran the City of Hope Christmas party, persuading Mattel and Hasbro and other toy manufacturers to donate carloads of toys for the dying kids. In 1956, she decided to spice things up with an idea that everyone called a pipe dream. She telephoned Marlon Brando, fresh from *On the Waterfront* and *The Wild One*, to see if the world's hottest movie star would come to the party. She talked to his agent, who explained that Mr. Brando was a very busy man. She called again and again, and the agent said Brando didn't think he would be very good at cheering up sick kids. But a few days later, Mary was talking on the phone with someone at City of Hope, who suddenly went all gooey, "Oh my God, Marlon Brando's just arrived!" Brando rode up on a big motorcycle, right before Christmas, wearing his famous jeans in his famous way and stunning the staff at the hospital. He talked to the children and their families, posed for pictures, and signed autographs. Later he narrated a film for the hospital. The brooding rebel turned out to be the perfect Santa.

Mary always brought her own children to the hospital parties, and her oldest son, Jim, worked as a Santa's helper. He recalls one year, when he was ten, he told his mother how upset he was that many of the kids would never see another Christmas, and she told him, "You can cry afterward. But we want to give them a reason to feel good." Her determination to give them some moments of joy made a lasting impression on him.

Theresa remembers when she was about nine going to work with her mother one day. While making her rounds to the movie studios, Mary spotted a homeless man in the street. She reached into her purse, emptied her wallet, and clickety-clacked across the road in her high heels and her fancy work clothes. Theresa watched as Mary gave the man the money and held both his hands in hers. When she came back to the car, Theresa was relieved that her mother had gotten away safe from the man, whose ragged appearance scared her. But she also felt proud that her mother cared about him.

The Brenner house was always the most crowded and most fun in the neighborhood because Mary was, as Jim says now, "a giant magnet — everyone wanted to be at our house." There was always somebody coming and going with loads of this or that, and Mary always played games with the children or told them stories. Kathleen remembers making mud pies with her mother's best silver, and her mother not caring. The kids never knew what might happen next.

One day a neighbor showed up at the Brenners' front door, bleeding from the mouth. Her husband, a lawyer, had a habit of smacking his wife when he drank too much. Infuriated, Mary went to have a little talk with him. Some of the kids sneaked out and followed her as she marched down the street. She banged on the door, the husband answered, and the kids watched as Mary wagged her finger up into the face of the much taller man, backing him into the house and shouting about how he should be ashamed of himself. He then came to the Brenners' house, clearly upset and humbled, to apologize to his wife. That was a powerful lesson for the kids, as they recall, about the power of conviction over muscle.

Mary constantly exposed her children to life's tough realities, as her own father had done for her. She took them to orphanages and to see Mexican migrant workers in the fields. Once she even took them to a "White Power" rally, where angry white men wore swastikas and shouted Nazi slogans. Even though she knew it would be a bit frightening to her kids, that ugliness and hatred was something she wanted them to understand.

After one trip to the migrant worker fields, Jim told her that if he ever had fifty thousand dollars, he would give half of it to the poor. His mother said she was so proud of him, and Jim didn't think about it again. Then the next week, instead of his fifty-cent allowance, his mother gave him just a quarter. Jim protested: "Where's my other quarter?"

"Well, if you're willing to give half of your fifty thousand away, you might as well start now. I'll give this other quarter to the poor."

"But Mom, it's only twenty-five cents."

She didn't budge.

"If you don't want to give the half of what you've got now," she said, "you're definitely not going to give half of it later."

The children received regular checks on their birthdays from a wealthy family friend, and Mary started a family tradition. The kids would use that money to treat the whole family to dinner. Theresa remembers loving the chance to be the one treating and realizing that giving everyone a good time was even better than buying a new toy.

On holidays, the Brenner house always filled up with children from a local orphanage. Mary took her own kids to round up orphans for Easter dinners, Thanksgiving turkeys, Christmas days, or even her kids' birthday parties. Carl usually stuck around to say hello to the children and eat dinner, and then left to play golf or fly his airplane.

Carol remembers that at Christmas, Mary took the kids caroling in the neighborhood to collect donations. The kids spent the money they collected on trees, wreaths, and food for needy families, which they dropped off on their doorsteps. They would ring the doorbell and run off. Carol says the kids loved being included in their mother's charity work, and they thought it brought fun and excitement into the house.

"Our mother always told us that everybody is born for a reason, and it was clear to us that she was born to do this," her daughter Kathleen says.

Mary came to see the chill in her marriage as an opportunity. Because Carl didn't want much of her time, she had more time to spend writing letters or making phone calls. Some people she knew thought that her charity work, which was growing into a major enterprise, was an escape, a way to fill the space left by an empty marriage. But Mary saw it in a much more positive light.

"All those things that had always gnawed inside of me about people's suffering, I was able to do something about," she says. "I wasn't running away from Carl. I didn't turn to charity to fill an empty life, because my children filled me and I had my business and I knew that other people needed me. Charity is not a thing you do, it's love, it's who you become. I was the salesman for the poor."

Her father died on March 12, 1956. He was only fifty, but his heart had ailed him for years and one morning it just stopped. The family buried Joseph Clarke in Burbank, beside his wife Kathleen, who died twenty-six years earlier. Even though Mary knew his death was coming, when it happened, it shocked her. Her father had been her inspiration and her compass. He had told her he hoped she would take over his company someday, and just four hours after he died, she did. She was twenty-nine.

Mary's vision and ambition for her charity work kept expanding. She called U.S. government relief agencies, church groups, and a private charity, the Direct

Relief Foundation, which helped her ratchet up her collection and worldwide distribution of American castoffs. Hospitals were gold mines. With the help of Cy Shulman, director of City of Hope, she began gathering unwanted goods from hospitals all over California. They had storage rooms filled with literally tons of medical supplies they would never use. When a new product or medicine came on the market, nobody wanted the old stuff anymore, even if it was still perfectly good. She discovered that they threw away dental equipment and medicine desperately sought in poorer countries. She sent donated hospital beds for a new hospital in Korea, while donated wheelchairs, bedpans, and other equipment went to Peru, the Philippines, and Guatemala.

She started running a block-long warehouse in Los Angeles for Direct Relief Foundation, which both exhilarated and exhausted her. She had no office, no secretary, and no staff. When the work seemed too overwhelming, she would sneak outside late at night and smoke cigarettes to take the edge off her nerves.

Her life was a blur of wake-ups, breakfast, school buses, work, and budgets and clients, then dinners, homework, baths, and bedtime.

Carl helped a little with the work at home, but he usually had somewhere else to be, often at his job as a sports supervisor at the L.A. Board of Education. Jim recalls that he would sometimes wake up at night and hear his mother in the next room still doing work. One night he saw her sitting at the family's big dining room table, with a pen in her hand and stacks of bills spread out all around her, crying.

She was still running her father's business, as he had wanted. But her heart was in her work for the poor. As she spent long sleepless nights with her son Tom, who suffered from asthma, Mary sometimes wondered if she was pushing too hard, if she could really hold together her family, her work, her volunteering, and what was left of her marriage.

Carl thought Mary's charity efforts were naïve. Their sharp political differences were highlighted by the tumult of the 1960s. Carl was Nixon; she was Kennedy. Theresa says it was like growing up with Barbra Streisand and Robert Redford in *The Way We Were*. Carl called Mary a left-wing radical, a pinko-commie, especially when she talked about her anger that the U.S. government was backing dictators such as Nicaragua's Anastasio Somoza and the Dominican Republic's General Rafael Trujillo. He saw them as stalwarts holding the line against communism, while Mary saw them as brutal dictators. She drove around with Kennedy-Johnson bumper stickers on her car and had her kids pass out campaign flyers and tell people to vote for the Democratic senator from Massachusetts. Jim remembers going to a big Kennedy rally at the Los Angeles Coliseum with her and singing along as the band played "When Irish Eyes Are Smiling." He went down on the floor and got close enough to get a handshake from Kennedy and then went days without washing that hand.

Mary vividly remembers one morning in the mid-1960s when she found herself distraught. Carl was particularly angry with her over all the time she was spending on charity, and she remembers praying, "Lord, maybe I'm devoting too much time to this work for the poor. Enlighten me. Let me hear from you, let me know."

As she was getting dressed for work, the phone rang. It was someone from Direct Relief Foundation, saying that they were in desperate need of several pediatric incubators for a hospital in Guatemala. Mary said she would see what she could do, and she began thinking about where she might find incubators. Less than an hour later, she was getting into her car when she heard the phone ring again. She ran back inside and answered it.

"Are you Mary Brenner?" the caller asked. "Are you the one who's helping send materials to needy countries?"

She said she was, and the man identified himself as someone from a hospital in San Pedro, near Los Angeles. He said they were closing down a pediatric ward of the hospital, and they had five almost-new incubators they wanted to donate.

"I don't know why God answered me so fast and so clearly," she says. "But he did."

Mary was sure that the phone call was a gift from God, a little shot of reassurance. And amid all the strains in her life, she also believes she was sent another such gift: the friendship of a priest who would be the inspiration for the way she would spend the rest of her life.

His name was Monsignor Anthony Brouwers, and he was a Los Angeles priest well known for his devotion to missionary causes. He had founded several groups, including Lay Mission Helpers, which sent and supported missionaries and doctors overseas. Brouwers had a special passion for Africa, and he organized groups of doctors to go there. He also wrote a column in a Catholic newspaper that Mary read avidly, and one day in 1957 she breezed into his office without an appointment. She felt she already knew him from his writings, and even though he was a very busy and important man in the church, she was sure he would see her, and he did.

Carrying photos of hungry children in Korea, Mary told Brouwers she didn't understand how God could allow such pain, rambling on about her own questions about God and the church, about how, truth be told, she didn't much care for all the church's rules and all that grim talk about sinners turning into pillars of salt. Don't get me wrong, she told him, she loved the church and she loved St. Anthony, Brouwers's namesake. Like millions of Catholics, she prayed to St. Anthony, who had somehow become the go-to saint when something was lost, even a set of car keys. But God disappointed and confused her, she said, by tolerating so much suffering, and frankly, if God loves us so much, why are there young Chinese boys dying in faraway ditches, their legs being eaten away by gangrene?

Brouwers, dressed in black with his

white Roman collar, listened patiently and fixed his brown eyes on her through his thick-rimmed glasses. At first he had pegged her for just another well-dressed socialite, but as she spoke he saw something more. Her directness and passion for the poor intrigued him.

"You're thinking the right way, Mary," he told her. He spoke about the God he believed in, a generous and kind and loving God. Men start wars, he said, and their lack of mercy and indifference is why children die of hunger. He invited her to come whenever she wanted to talk about charity work and the church, including those pesky rules that bothered her so. Then he said a simple sentence that filled her with happiness, and even relief, in the face of her doubts about her church and her faith: "Mary, you'll never be an atheist."

She took him up on his offer and visited him again. The two shared an intellectual and spiritual bond. They both believed they had a responsibility to ease the suffering of those born into poverty, and her talks with him rejuvenated her faith. "Mary, your love for the poor is supernatural," he told her. It meant a lot to her when such a church luminary told her she was "a good woman, a holy woman," despite the stigma of divorce in the eyes of the church.

As she came to know him better, Mary turned to Brouwers with her personal problems. She told him about her dying marriage and that she felt like a woman tied to railroad tracks with a train bearing down on her. He told her to keep faith and God would help her through. Brouwers embodied what Mary loved most about the Catholic Church. He lived to help others, and he inspired her to do the same. When she and Carl had their last child together, in 1961, she named him Anthony, in honor of Brouwers, who baptized the boy.

Mary had a silver-blue mink, which she wore for special events. It was worth about eighteen hundred dollars and had been given to her as a Christmas present years earlier by her company. She adored it. She felt beautiful when she wore it. It was a little bit of the old Hollywood glitz from her childhood. But in the growing world of her charity work, the stole seemed like a shameful luxury.

So on Christmas Eve 1961, she brought it to Brouwers to raffle off for his overseas missions. She had it cleaned, and as she folded it into a lovely box, she felt a tear falling from her eye. That fur was the only thing she ever owned that she felt pain about giving up. But when a wealthy church parishioner paid eight thousand dollars for it, she realized she was on to something. She later bought and raffled several more minks and raised enough money to build a wing on a hospital in the southern African nation of Malawi, which was named for Brouwers. From then on, she couldn't see women wearing a mink or a string of pearls and not think to herself, "Don't you know you're wearing a hospital around your neck?"

Mary's relationship with Brouwers made a profound impression on her that strengthened her faith and her belief in her calling to charity. In 1963, spinal cancer left Brouwers permanently confined to a hospital bed. The cancer had eaten away at his nerves and spine and left him partially paralyzed. He continued to write and organize missionary work from his bed, and Mary visited him constantly. She usually arrived at his bedside very late at night when he couldn't sleep and her children were already asleep.

They talked about missionary work, the endless needs of the poor, God, and what drove them. Those were deeply emotional talks for Mary, who had never been so inspired by anyone, except perhaps her own father.

"Do you see why you are where you are?" Brouwers told her one night, just before his death in 1964. "That little cottage that you wanted to go away to and make Toll House cookies. That wasn't meant for you. This was meant for you. The front lines. God put you in that role, Mary."

His words would soon take on new meaning for her, when she discovered a place that drew her as none ever had.

FOUR

BECOMING MOTHER

A year after Monsignor Brouwers died, Mary answered a phone call that changed her life.

Father Henry Vetter, a priest from Pasadena who did missionary work in Mexico, called to say he had heard about her considerable efforts for the poor. He invited her to come with him on a trip to Tijuana, where there was more need than she could imagine. So they made a date to set off with a carload of supplies and medicine in 1965, and after visiting a couple of local hospitals, they ended up at the gate of La Mesa state penitentiary. They didn't have an appointment, but the warden said they could take their donations to the prison infirmary.

Past the barbed wire and high concrete walls, past the watchtowers with armed soldiers, they walked into the pulsing world of the prison. Almost immediately Mary saw a handcuffed prisoner, which brought back painful memories of how she'd felt during the births of her first four children, when the nurses put straps on her arms to hold her down.

Hundreds of prisoners jammed the prison, which covered a city block. A few rich drug traffickers lived in well-equipped prison apartments, while poor petty thieves scrounged for places to sleep. Mexico, like many poor countries, did not provide food and beds for all its inmates, and prisoners had to pay for everything from water to toilet paper. They relied on their families to provide for them, but not everyone had money or family. As Mary entered that first day, women were lined up outside the front gate, toting whole chickens and little propane stoves to cook them on, clothes, and blankets. Less-savory items were smuggled in as well, sometimes by visitors, and sometimes by way of the "rain of objects," when drugs and guns were stuffed into soccer balls and tossed over the walls to waiting inmates.

Father Vetter and Mary strolled into *El Pueblito* — the little village — the prison's Main Street, a chaotic jumble of jury-rigged wood and cinder block buildings in the prison's central courtyard. There prisoners created little wooden stands selling tamales and tacos. Many sported signs painted to look like the logos of famous eateries. The fanciest *carracas* had separate bedrooms and fully stocked tequila bars. Rich inmates ordered in dinner from their favorite restaurants in San Diego and kept themselves well supplied with liquor, clothes, and women.

Mary and Father Vetter walked past the communal cell where new prisoners were held, many of them ragged, still in the filthy clothes they had been arrested in. She thought the inmates looked more sad than dangerous. They called out to her and Vetter in Spanish, but she had no idea what they were saying, so she smiled at them with as much cheeriness as she could muster.

In the prison infirmary, they found virtually no medicine. Sick prisoners lay on the floor because there were not enough cots, and when they saw the visitors — one a priest, the other a well-dressed foreign woman — they stood up out of respect. Mary told them to lie back down, and she felt drawn to help them. Of everything she had seen in the prison, the poorly equipped infirmary made the most lasting impression.

"They just looked like sick people," she

94

says. "Poor, yes. But I didn't see anyone I'd be afraid to talk to. I thought, This is a poor place — not fearful, not dark, not dangerous. Just poor."

That first visit to La Mesa affected her so profoundly that even though Tijuana was at least a three-hour drive from her home in Los Angeles, she started visiting regularly, often with another Maryknoll priest, Father Elmer Wurth. Hers were the only fresh bandages and warm words that many of the prisoners ever received. On each visit, she learned more and more about the life of the prison and the stories of the prisoners' lives. Many were from Central America, desperate migrants who set off to find work in the United States but found themselves detoured to La Mesa for a thousand sad reasons. Some hacked with tuberculosis and ached from neglect, infections, and stabbings.

Over the months, and eventually the years, Mary became a familiar figure at La Mesa. Her lack of Spanish limited her interactions with inmates, but she tried to communicate with gestures. "Kindness is a visit. A smile is a visit. Reaching out and holding somebody's hand is a visit," she says. The guards helped her carry the goods she brought, the warden told her to come back whenever she wanted, and the inmates crowded around her. On one visit, a prisoner greeted her with a poem he had written for her: "You have come here like a beautiful rose. You will leave, but your fragrance will remain here for a very long time." She found the graciousness almost overwhelming.

She heard about the prison's darker side as well. She knew there was a place called F Tank, where mentally ill inmates were warehoused in horrible conditions. She heard complaints from prisoners about the *Grito,* a brutal three-day initiation rite for newly arrived prisoners. There were mentions of punishment cells, from which prisoners often emerged with their teeth smashed out, and an old gymnasium where they were "interrogated." But she was still an honored day guest in the prison, and most of the dirty laundry of the place was kept from her.

She remembers being cold all the time when she visited, because the prison wasn't heated. Decades later, she has become so used to the cold that she can't stand to be in heated rooms; she can actually smell the heat, and it feels suffocating to her.

Determined to improve conditions at La Mesa, she started coming over the border with truckloads of supplies, including mattresses the U.S. Navy base in San Diego discarded by the hundreds. She also brought large quantities of perfectly wrapped hamburgers that were about to be thrown away by U.S. fast-food restaurants at the end of the day. She would charm border guards who were intrigued that this pretty American woman was hauling supplies to a Mexican prison.

When she wasn't in La Mesa, concerns about the inmates filled her thoughts more and more. When it rained, she wondered if they were warm and had blankets. She wondered who had been locked away in punishment cells, or if everyone had enough food. She wondered if they had clothes. She could never get them out of her mind.

One night in 1969 she had a dream so vivid that she shot out of bed to write it down. She was a prisoner about to be executed, and Christ came to take her place. She was sure the dream was about La Mesa and how she should be coming to the aid of the most desperate prisoners. That dream reinforced her sense that she was meant to be at La Mesa, where she had come to feel at home. She felt most like herself when she was there, more energized and more vital.

As her commitment to La Mesa grew, her interest in her work at her father's company faded. When the Vietnam War began, defense contractors were still her biggest accounts, and even though she sold them only carbon paper and office supplies, she felt somehow complicit in the mounting death toll in Southeast Asia. The war appalled her, and the worse it got, the more friction that caused with Carl. They argued about it constantly. He told her vital American interests were at stake, but she saw nothing but senseless death and suffering. The class divisions of the war especially offended her. While the wealthy won deferments for college or for some slight or invented medical problem, she saw Hispanic names filling the daily list of the war dead in the *Los Angeles Times*.

Her friends told her she was selling carbon paper, not dropping bombs, but nonetheless she felt like part of the war machine. So in 1970, while thousands of protestors carried peace signs in the streets, Mary made her own quiet demonstration, and with a nod to her long-dead father, she closed the business. She knew he wouldn't have objected.

The next two years were unhappy ones,

as Mary became more and more disillusioned with her marriage and she and Carl barely spoke anymore. Even about something as important as shutting her father's business, he was simply indifferent, telling her, "If that's what you want to do, it's your life." For so many years she had forced herself not to think about divorce because of the kids. But she knew the current situation wasn't good for them, either, and finally she decided the marriage had to end.

In 1972, Carl moved out of the Granada Hills house and took an apartment. No particular fight or incident caused him to leave. She had been pressuring him to move out; she can't even remember exactly what was said on the day he finally did. They were divorced not long after, and a few months later, at the age of forty-five, Mary sold the house and moved to an apartment in Ventura, a few blocks from the beach, with a deck that looked out over a marina. Her older children were already grown and gone, and she was sure that on her own she could take care of her two youngest, Elizabeth, who was thirteen, and eleven-year-old Anthony.

Mary was deeply depressed over the failure of her second marriage. She took long walks on the Ventura beach with her German shepherd, Guy, and thought about what had gone wrong and what she might have done differently. Mulling over the years with Carl, she thought she probably could have made life work with him if she had tried harder. She second-guessed herself about the kind of wife she had been, and whether she had devoted more passion and caring to poor children on the other side of the world than to her own marriage. The divorce seemed to her an enormous failure, to herself, to Carl, to her family, and to her church.

Still in her forties, she had many years ahead of her, and she felt at a crossroads in her life. She felt blessed that she had her seven healthy children and that they were such a source of joy for her. But she was done with marriage. She walked and walked on the beach, thinking and praying, trying to figure out what to do with her life. During those long walks, she kept thinking about what Brouwers had told her, that she was meant for charity work on the front lines. She had often daydreamed about being a missionary as a child, and now she realized she could actually do it.

She had started taking Holy Communion again. According to church rules, she was permitted to because she was no longer living with a man other than her husband. In the church's eyes, she was still married to Ray but separated from him. Now back on better terms with the church, she wondered if she might be able to pursue her missionary dream as a Catholic sister. She had no desire to be a cloistered nun in a convent, but she thought she would fit well in an order that worked among the poor. Because of her family's association with the Maryknolls, she made inquiries about joining them, but they did not accept anyone older than thirty-five. She learned that religious orders wanted only young women because older women tend to become sick and be more of a burden than a help. Once again, she thought her church's rules ran counter to its true purposes. Closing the door to older women asking to devote their lives to serving the church just seemed wrong. They were not welcoming of divorced women, either, and Mary began thinking that she would have to change that.

Having been turned down by established orders, she started contemplating a truly bold idea: What if she moved into La Mesa as a sort of independent sister? She had been going there on and off for more than a decade, and every time she left, she had the nagging feeling she was letting someone down, leaving behind someone who needed her. Her visits there had begun to seem insufficient, like trying to satisfy hunger with cotton candy. Seeing her at the prison working late at night, the warden had told her she was welcome to stay over whenever she wanted. She thought maybe she should take him up on his offer.

Mary wrestled with the idea, and the more she thought about it, the more she wanted to do it. She finally made the decision on Easter Sunday 1976. Her family had gathered in her Ventura home, except for Carl, who had remarried. All of her kids came, along with her six grandchildren at the time, dressed in bonnets and bright spring colors and loaded down with Easter eggs and candies. As Mary surveyed her happy family, in a moment of striking clarity, she said a quiet prayer, "Thank you, God. You've given me so many years and so many feasts like this. But this is the last one for me. This is the last time that I am going to spend Easter like this. I am going to be with you next year. I am going to the prison. I am going to where I am being led." She had never been so sure of anything, and she felt as though she had reached a place that she had been walking toward for a very long time.

She had made her choice; she was going to wear a habit — even if that had to be without the church's official sanction — and she was going to move into La Mesa. She wouldn't be able to move in full-time right away; her youngest two children, Elizabeth and Anthony, still lived at home. So for a while at least she'd have to commute back and forth, but after that, she would sell her house and make La Mesa her permanent home.

Her children weren't the slightest bit surprised when she told them her plans. "We had seen it coming our whole life," says her daughter Kathleen, who said it seemed so natural that she doesn't recall any of her brothers and sisters even discussing it among themselves. Kathleen says she encouraged her mother. "We were so used to that," she says. "My mother, from the time we were babies, used to grab towels and pin them on the back of our heads as veils. We played nun all the time."

She began giving away her possessions and making other preparations for the transition, arranging for a neighbor to stay at her house for a night or two a week to

103

watch Anthony, who was fifteen, on nights that she would spend at the prison. Her daughter Elizabeth was almost eighteen and was about to marry Ron Blair, the bass player in the hugely popular rock band Tom Petty and the Heartbreakers.

It was time to go.

On March 19, 1977, Mary Brenner woke up in her house in Ventura and slipped on a simple long-sleeved black dress and a black veil that she sewed herself, which she thought looked "nunny." Then she stood before the mirror and disappeared.

The woman looking back at her was Mother Antonia.

She chose the name in honor of Anthony Brouwers. Cancer had taken him far too young, but his work and his name, or at least a Spanish female version of it, would now live on through her. As she looked at herself in the habit for the first time, she saw someone she had known for a lifetime. She felt wonderful and natural and thought, "This is who I am."

She felt she should wear a habit because it was an important symbol of her faith and of the missionary tradition she was following. She also thought it was important for her to be at La Mesa around the clock.

Riots often started at night, stabbings and shootings tended to happen in the dark, and sick prisoners had no one else to turn to after doctors went home for the day. She wanted to be there when her help was most needed.

The act was audacious, she knew, a show of sheer will. She belonged to no order, and she didn't have the church's formal approval. But she had never put rules ahead of faith, and she wouldn't start now. She had spoken with priests and sisters she admired, and they had encouraged her. She felt it was the work she was meant to be doing. It wasn't like she could go to the bishop's office and pick up a job application for "American nun in Mexican prison." The job didn't exist. And even if it did, she wouldn't qualify because of her divorces, so she blazed her own trail. An American housewife could bring donated clothing and be appreciated by the prisoners in La Mesa, but a Catholic sister would be far more trusted.

She believed down to her toes that God had chosen this life for her and that He had been shouting his plan to her for years. Father Vetter, the priest who had introduced her to La Mesa, encouraged her to go to Our Lady of the Assumption church in Ventura, where she used to go to Mass every morning, and make personal vows. Wearing the Maryknoll medallion around her neck that Sister Angelica had worn for fifty years, she knelt and made silent vows of obedience, chastity, fidelity, and service. Those vows didn't have the weight of the church behind them, but Mary figured that if she and God had an understanding, nothing else really mattered.

Walking out to her car, she felt in a way an impostor in her new religious clothes, but an honest servant in her heart. She drove south through San Diego, past the beautiful bay filled with sails puffed full of warm spring breezes, on smooth wide roads to the border. When she crossed into Tijuana, she drove past honky-tonk bars and down roads narrower than the runways on the aircraft carriers tied up in San Diego. At every intersection, there were clutches of poor men, women, and children selling candies and hoping for a peso. She parked at General Hospital. Just hours after she had been looking at herself in the mirror in Ventura, she was now looking at four Mexican policemen.

She had been to the hospital before to bring donations and visit the sick, but now she was nervous. This was a first stop on her way to the prison, a warm-up lap. In the crowded entryway, she smiled to cover her fear: Would somebody call her bluff? As sick people passed her, she made the sign of the cross to bless them. One of the police officers standing just inside the doorway called her over. *Uh-oh,* she thought, *I'm caught.* She was sure the cops knew she wasn't authorized to wear the habit. What were they going to do? She thought for a second that maybe she had misinterpreted the signs from God, and that He had sent the police to straighten out the misunderstanding.

But the officers smiled at her warmly. *"Y nosotros?"* one said. Aren't you going to bless us, too, *Madre?* So she blessed them with the sign of the cross, and they thanked her. She wanted to dance down the hall, because she had her answer. She was on her way.

She drove to La Mesa and walked through the gate carrying a blanket, a pillow, a Spanish dictionary, and a Bible. As she passed inside, a sudden thought made her smile: no more shopping for clothes or spending money in a beauty shop. She still had her apartment in Ventura, but she had given away nearly all her possessions and she delighted in what she called her new freedom of nonownership.

"I knew that I had been an outsider to suffering all my life," she says. "I'd been on the outside helping people on the inside, whether it was in Africa or Bolivia or anywhere else. All of a sudden it occurred to me, when I step over that line and walk through that door, I become an insider with them. I don't just work for them, I am one with them. I live the way they live. Once you're on the inside it's so different. I felt that I had joined the suffering. Somehow the prison was the place where I finally experienced the freedom to be myself, to really be myself. I think prison freed me."

She walked down a narrow corridor to the office of the warden, who told her he was delighted to have her stay over. She explained that her plan was to stay a night or two each week at first, then gradually build up to moving in full-time, although she wasn't sure exactly when that would be. She would be commuting from her home in Ventura, where she was living with Anthony. The warden offered to find Mother Antonia a private corner of the prison where she could sleep, but she insisted on a place in the crowded female cell block, a large room filled with triple-decker bunk beds, and she walked in and dropped her few things on the empty middle bunk.

"Having seven kids you can sleep any-place, so sleeping in a bunk was not a sacrifice to me. I was happy about it," she says. "I didn't feel any fear. I didn't worry if this was the right thing. In the Old Testament it says, 'He who puts the hand on the plough and looks back isn't worthy of service.' So once I put my hand on the plough, I wasn't going to look back. I could only go ahead."

The other inmates were curious and asked who she was visiting. She told them that she was staying full-time. *"Es mi casa, es mi casa."* This is my home, she told them. "I'm going to stay here with you, I'm going to share life with you." The women were startled and began offering her blankets, coffee, a little food — any-thing she needed.

On her first night, inmates slept in the bunk above her and below her. She changed into her nightclothes under her blanket, trying not to bang her head in the tiny space. When she woke up the next morning, she saw a pair of men's boots on the floor. The woman above her was sleeping with her husband or boyfriend, and Mother Antonia decided to be more careful from then on about staying over on nights when conjugal visits were allowed. It would take some time to get the hang of life in La Mesa.

In her first weeks, she immersed herself in Spanish and listened to records and tapes until she mastered the basics. She asked a lot of questions and quickly began amusing inmates and guards with her command of Mexican street slang. The same woman who used to run her fingers along windowsills to check for dust in her Beverly Hills living room now lived in a prison with rats, nasty smells, and nastier graffiti. She began learning every purple word from the mouths of street toughs. The change in her life was exciting and she felt, maybe for the first time, there was no place else in the world where she would rather be.

Nobody made any formal announcement that Mother Antonia was in the prison; she just began showing up more and more often. Gradually her story became just another part of the eclectic La Mesa mix, and she settled in to her work. Every day she brought food and blankets and medicine and spent hours in the infirmary holding hands with prisoners in pain. She also began trying to win the trust of guards, men like Apolinar Aguilar Nieto, who remembers how she would step right into the middle of violent confrontations.

"There was a lot of physical violence, and she acted as an intermediary," recalls Aguilar, who remains friendly with Mother Antonia almost thirty years later. "She calmed both the guards and the inmates, it was very brave of her to risk her life by getting involved in disputes."

Anthony Solano, a top prison administrator when Mother Antonia first arrived, remembers her as "a tornado of energy, working from five in the morning until long after I left at eight p.m. I would turn off my light and she would still be there, bringing materials as well as affection."

Her children were supportive about her prison work, and many of them came to visit her in La Mesa. Her daughter Kathleen says she and her siblings had always known that their mother wasn't a typical mom.

One day, shortly after Mother Antonia put on the habit for the first time, she paid a surprise visit to her son Jim, who was about thirty and living with his wife close to San Diego. She walked up to the front door and knocked. Jim opened the door and found his mother standing there wearing a habit. She spun around like a model on a runway.

"Well, whaddya think?" she said.

Seeing his mother in the habit for the first time, he says, was like seeing Cinderella's foot in the glass slipper. It made sense. "You know, you look great," Jim told her. "But I've seen you that way my whole life."

Her children understood what a positive change this was for their mother, but for the first year, her routine of commuting back and forth to the prison took a toll on her son Anthony, who turned sixteen in the summer of 1977 and was the only one left at home. He became increasingly worried for her safety, and he wanted her to spend more time with him.

The divorce had been the hardest on Anthony. He still felt hurt and angry at his parents over their split, and now on top of all of that, he had to cope with a mother who had taken to wearing a nun's habit. Later that year, the two of them moved from Ventura to an apartment in San Diego to be closer to Tijuana, which was another disruption for him. Anthony understood what his mother was doing; he had been going with her to the prison since he was about ten, helping her carry donated goods and distributing them to the prisoners. But he still worried about her. He could see her part-time work becoming not just full-time, but permanent, and La Mesa scared him. He was bothered by the violence there and was upset when he first saw the grim little place where she slept. To him, it didn't look like a home. She seemed all alone.

"I was hurt, and I was fearful," says Anthony, now in his forties, married, and running a clothing business in Irvine, California. He had seen her go through the pain of divorce, and now seeing her in La Mesa, he felt bad for her.

"I saw my dad go on and get remarried, and he had his own life," he says. "My brothers and sisters, they had their lives, they were married. Everyone was on their own and taken care of, and my mom was by herself. She was doing this work in Mexico that was really hard. I wanted her to find somebody to love her."

Mother Antonia was distressed about how much Anthony worried about her, and she increasingly had to acknowledge that the awkward arrangement wasn't good for him. She cried and worried and prayed about it. She wanted to be in the prison, but she also wanted Anthony to be happy and to be a good mother to him.

Anthony still had a good relationship

with Carl. On the weekends they spent together, they passed long hours on the golf course. A promising young player, Anthony had inherited his father's athletic ability, and he hoped to play professionally someday. Golf served as the common ground where Anthony and his father made peace about the divorce.

Though Mother Antonia did not want to give up primary custody of Anthony, she began to realize it would be the best thing for him. She read as much as she could about the effects of divorce on children, especially adolescent boys. Everything was telling her that Anthony would be fine with his father, maybe even better off. Still, the move was agonizing for her: Anthony would spend the week with his father and the weekends with her in San Diego. It was the hardest decision she ever made.

"I was a basket case," she says.

Knowing that her decision might be hard for others to understand, she says, "If I did just what other people thought I should do, I would never have gone to La Mesa. When you know in your heart that something is right, that it's who you are, that God is calling you to do something, you make the sacrifices you have to make."

Anthony said that even as a teenager he

gradually realized that his mother had made the right choice. After he was living with his father, he remembers visiting his mother regularly in La Mesa over the next years. "I would see the prisoners call her Mama, and part of me would say, 'Wait a minute, she's my mama,'" he says. "But then I would think, 'This is really good for her. This is where she needs to be.'"

These days Anthony loves to brag about her accomplishments. He sees her often and talks to her regularly on the phone, as do all of her children. Their relationship is warm and close. "I don't think I ever had resentment toward my mother at all," he says. "I went through some pain at sixteen or seventeen. But at the end of the day, for what my mom's achieved in the past twenty-some years, I would have gone through a heck of a lot more. Believe me.

"I'm pretty religious, so today I look back and I really think I've been blessed. There was sacrifice there as a young man, I see it clearly. But then there's that saying, 'Get over it!' And that's where I am. I thank God I have my mother and the work that she's done. And I really feel so special today because of that."

In March 1978, after a year of spending more and more nights in La Mesa, Mother

Antonia sold her place in San Diego and moved into the prison for good. All her children still live in Southern California, except for Elizabeth, who lives in Texas. She talks to them often and sees them regularly. "I have never felt that my mother was more than a phone call away," says Theresa, a labor administrator in the California state government. "She never stopped being our mom."

FIVE

LEARNING THE ROPES

Mother Antonia slept in the women's cell block for months before the warden gave her a *carraca* of her own.

It was a tiny place, which some of the guards joked was no bigger than a dining room table. But having a little private space made things a bit easier. As she began establishing herself in the prison, she felt it was important that no one ever see her without her habit or in her night-gown, and that posed a problem when she had to go to the bathroom in the middle of the night. Her cell had no toilet, and when she was too exhausted to get up and get dressed and find the communal bathroom, she urinated in a jar.

As the months wore on, she got used to doing without the comforts she had lived with for decades. She no longer even noticed when dinner was a can of green beans warmed with hot water from her little coffeepot. Prison slang didn't show up in the Spanish lessons in her tapes and books, and she often had no idea what people were saying. She focused on practical needs that needed no translation: the lack of milk or medicine, a shirt, or a sandwich. She felt lucky that she was living in a place where everywhere she turned, there was someone who needed her help. And now that she was there all day and all night, she was finding much to love about the men and women who had landed in La Mesa, most of them for the smallest of crimes.

Some prisoners, who so desperately wanted out of La Mesa, couldn't believe she had chosen to live there and they invented wild stories that flew around the prison. She must be an agent of the FBI or Drug Enforcement Administration (DEA); maybe she was some kind of Black Widow nun who had killed her husband and was now trying to make amends to God. The rumors persisted for years, and Mother Antonia once found herself having to convince a guard that her tiny cassette recorder was not for surreptitiously recording drug traffickers, but for playing love songs.

"My God, it really is Julio Iglesias," the guard said after she hit the PLAY button to prove it to him.

Mother Antonia ignored the gossip and focused on the needs. She saw inmates die from stabbings, gunshots, and disease, and when no one claimed their bodies, she buried them. She comforted many grieving prisoners whose children died while they were behind bars, and she arranged with the warden to bring the bodies into the prison for a last good-bye.

She found that the prison could be astonishingly humane in some ways. Prisoners were allowed to have conjugal visits, and family members could even move in if they chose to. Every morning the prison gate teemed with wives and girlfriends fixing their makeup on their way to work or children waiting for a school bus that stopped right at La Mesa's doorstep. Inmates booked the prison chapel for countless weddings, baptisms, and funerals, and family members from outside were welcome to attend.

For several years, La Mesa hosted a bustling casino, where rich inmates and high rollers from outside the prison came to play cards. They drank twenty-dollar bottles of beer and gambled thousands of dollars, with a hefty cut going to the drug traffickers who ran the casino and the prison officials who allowed it to exist. Amid all the chaos and violence, inmates found comfort in a sense of normal family life, and even a little bit of Vegas nightlife.

But most of those comforts were for inmates with money. Conditions were miserable for the poor, especially the mentally ill. In those days, they were kept apart from the others, as though they were rotten apples that might poison the barrel. In La Mesa, they dumped them in F Tank. It was little more than a pen, separated from the rest of the prison by fencing and barbed wire. There was a roof of sorts over parts of it, but much of it was open to the rain, and the floor was mainly dirt. It usually was crammed with sixty or seventy men, many of them convicted of violent crimes. When it rained, the ground and the men were covered with mud. The toilet was a corner of the pen where human waste piled up. Heavily armed guards in a special tower watched over F Tank. When Mother Antonia first saw it, she was shocked and began a campaign to improve conditions there.

Late at night in her *carraca,* she sometimes would hear screams of men being "investigated" in a converted gym upstairs. She would run up and plead with the guards to stop the abuse and to abolish the punishment cells.

On one of her very first days in La Mesa, a group of men viciously beat a prisoner jailed for rape and dropped him like a sack of rocks on the infirmary's concrete floor. Mother Antonia heard that he was there and rushed up to see if she could help him. She found him lying where he had been dropped, bleeding and unable to move. When she knelt down next to him, a guard told her not to bother because he was a rapist and deserved what he got. Ignoring him, she tried to wash the man's wounds with a rag. She began praying the Hail Mary, and when she couldn't remember the Spanish words, the injured prisoner finished the prayer for her. The guard looked down at her with tears in his eyes. He helped her pick the man up, lay him on a hospital bed, and wash off the blood. It was an early victory in a long crusade to persuade the guards to be more humane.

Many new prisoners arrived at La Mesa with stories — and bruises and scars — of the mistreatment they suffered in police stations or local jails on their way to the state penitentiary. So Mother Antonia began making regular trips to those jails and to nearby police headquarters. She talked her way into regular visits with the men and women locked up there, showering blessings and goodies on both the jailers and the jailed.

She saw an unending need for basic necessities. She could help hundreds of people every day if she could simply keep a steady supply of medicine, clothes, and food coming into the prison. She knew right where to find them: Across the border from Tijuana lay the richest state in America.

In a San Diego junkyard, she found old toilets that she brought back to replace the smashed ones in the prison. Mercy Hospital in San Diego was renovating and gave her old beds and shelves, and pharmacies were happy to give her samples of aspirins and other medicines.

In the summer of 1977, Mother Antonia walked into the Popular Market, a grocery store in downtown San Diego, where Jesse González stood working the cash register. She asked if the store would donate a case of toilet paper for prisoners in Tijuana. People came to his store all the time asking for donations, and he regularly gave them beans, rice, or bread. But nobody had ever asked for toilet paper, and nobody had asked for anything for prisoners. He thought her request was odd, but he agreed.

Mother Antonia thanked Jesse and walked back out into the hot streets, heading for the next store. After she came in once or twice more, he couldn't resist asking her why she wanted toilet paper instead of food.

"Have you ever gone to the bathroom and tried to clean yourself when you don't have any toilet paper? How would you feel?" she asked him. He said he had never considered the poor's bathroom needs, and the fact that she had impressed him. Especially because she was an American caring for Mexicans whom even most Mexicans didn't care about, he wanted to get to know her better.

As he did, Jesse, who was born in Mexico, decided to do everything he could to help her. Mother Antonia took him on a tour of the prison, and he couldn't sleep for three nights afterward. She brought him to the holding cell where new prisoners were kept, a room forty feet long and twenty feet across, holding about sixty men the day Jesse came to visit. Jesse had brought sandwiches and apples from the market, and the prisoners gulped them down in seconds. He couldn't believe the terrible conditions or that she lived there.

Jesse became one of Mother Antonia's

early advocates in San Diego. He started taking her around the neighborhood at 12th and Broadway, where the Popular Market is located. The market was the tough barrio's center of gravity; everybody came in at some point to buy cigarettes or beer or groceries, and everybody knew Jesse. He stopped people on the street, introduced her, and explained her work. He also brought her into the neighborhood's shops and bars. Pretty soon the quarters and dollars were pulled off the bar and thrown into the hat. Many of the people in the neighborhood were Mexicans themselves, and they could imagine all too well what La Mesa must be like.

Jesse and the market's owner, Sam Barr, made up stamped envelopes addressed to Sister Antonia, in care of the Popular Market, and left them in businesses all over the neighborhood. Small donations started pouring in, and people dropped off bags filled with old clothes. The market became a busy collection spot for Mother Antonia's fledgling mission.

Every week Mother Antonia's work seemed to become better known, and she attracted an increasingly diverse group of people who wanted to help her.

Something clicked when Noreen Walsh-

Begun met Mother Antonia that same summer. Noreen had traveled the world and fallen in love with yogurt on a backpacking trip to Iran. One thing led to another, and now she owned Yogurt World, a little San Diego shop selling a new idea called frozen yogurt to trendy Californians. Mother Antonia come in to Noreen's shop as she made her rounds looking for donations, and the next thing Noreen knew, she was touring La Mesa.

Noreen didn't know exactly why, but she needed to help Mother Antonia help the prisoners. She was drawn to Mother Antonia's uncommonly strong presence. Noreen had heard an expression: It's not learning that brings you to perfection, it's unlearning. But she had never fully understood what that meant until she met Mother Antonia. Noreen thought that by giving up all her money and possessions to go work in the prison, Mother Antonia had "unlearned" one way of life and started a better one. Noreen wanted to be part of it.

Yogurt World, like the Popular Market, became a clearinghouse for Mother Antonia's collection efforts in San Diego. People brought garbage bags full of used clothes, food, medicine, blankets, toys, sheets, and other goods that Noreen stacked up in a back room. She talked up Mother Antonia to her customers, who told their friends, who mentioned her to their neighbors. The shoe repair shop next door donated all the old shoes nobody wanted or forgot to pick up. The flower shop gave Noreen day-old flowers for Mother Antonia to take to hospital patients in Tijuana. Yogurt World won the neighborhood Christmas decoration contest, and instead of taking the prize — a trip to Palm Springs — Noreen raffled it off and gave the two hundred dollars it raised to Mother Antonia's mission.

Noreen never knew what Mother Antonia would come up with next. One morning she called and asked Noreen if she would mind picking up Archie Moore, the sixty-eight-year-old boxing legend who had fought both Rocky Marciano and Muhammad Ali. He had agreed to Mother Antonia's request to come to La Mesa to cheer up the prisoners. Many inmates loved to box, and Mother Antonia knew how a visit from Moore would lift their spirits. Moore, who knocked out more opponents in his career than anyone else in boxing history, got into the prison ring and showed the prisoners some moves, sparring lightly with a few of them and bringing a day of rare joy to the prison.

Noreen occasionally stayed over in the prison with Mother Antonia, which exhausted her because Mother Antonia slept so little. They rose early and worked late, never stopping. Mother Antonia would mean to head back to her *carraca* to go to bed, but along the way she would stop to talk to a guard or a prisoner and the conversation would reenergize her. Then they'd be off for a cup of coffee and another hour of work.

Noreen frequently stayed over in Mother Antonia's cell, but not during the years when she lived in a cell directly over a place where raw sewage ran beneath the floor. Mother Antonia slept wearing a surgical mask to ward off the stench, which worsened during the rainy season when the sewer filled to the brim. Noreen thought no human being should have to live there, but Mother Antonia simply said that if the inmates had to live that way, she would, too.

Those who work with Mother Antonia often marvel at her willingness to ask anybody for anything. Her confidence in what she is doing, combined with her fast-talking powers of persuasion, make her, according to her friend Father Joe Carroll, the perfect street hustler.

One day, Carroll looked out his office window at the St. Vincent de Paul thrift shop on Market Street in downtown San Diego. He saw Mother Antonia piling up cartloads of used clothing, shoes, and other goods from the shop and loading them into her huge old 1979 Checker Cab, royal blue with a black roof, so big it seated twelve.

Carroll was furious. New in town and trying to get the little thrift shop off the ground, he had heard about the nun who had been coming to the shop and charming his staff into giving her huge loads of stuff to help prisoners in Mexico. Helpful was helpful, but what he saw out the window that day was just too much. So he ran down the stairs to put an end to it.

When he confronted her, she fell immediately to her knees.

"And she says in this really sweet voice," he recalls, " 'Padre, your blessing, please give me your blessing.' Meanwhile, my guys are loading up her car and my stuff's going out the door. What am I supposed to do — I'm a priest. So I said, 'Well of course, Sister, I'll bless you.' And she's holding my hand saying, 'You're so holy.'

Then once you look in her eyes, that's it. 'No' disappears from your vocabulary real quick."

Over the years, Father Joe, as everyone knows him, expanded his little thrift shop into Father Joe's Villages, a nonprofit giant that provides food, shelter, clothing, health care, and counseling to thousands every year. Honored as one of President George H. W. Bush's "points of light" and with the President's Service Award by President Bill Clinton, Carroll describes himself as the "hustler priest." He built his organization with street smarts he learned as a poor kid growing up in Brooklyn. He has courted the media, charmed rich donors with his Noo-Yawk tawk, and begged and borrowed to give to the poor. So it is with love and respect — and a great big belly laugh — that he bestows on Mother Antonia his highest compliment: "She's a thief! The best thief I've ever seen! A con woman, a hustler! She'll never stop picking your pocket. I'm a New Yorker, a wheeler-dealer. I'm the hustler priest. But she outhustles me every time."

For the past quarter-century, Father Joe's warehouses have been a prime source of the goods that Mother Antonia distributes in the prison — including mobile homes that she has turned into shelter for AIDS patients. Carroll jokes that every time he gets a phone call or an Easter card from her, his first reaction is, "Uh-oh, what's this going to cost me?

"I've never blessed anybody as much as I've blessed her," he says. "She'll come in here and say, 'Father, I need your blessing.' And then I hear the truck backing up."

Carroll loves to help her.

"You respond to her. She doesn't demand; she doesn't really ask. I mean, she'll ask in a way that you're not really being asked: 'Oh, I have all these children who have no pants. And I happened to be in the warehouse and saw this stack of pants . . .' And you give it to her because you're just happy you're able to do something for her. You walk away with more than you gave. You just feel like you've touched God a little bit.

"You sense this pure joy from her. And it's nice to touch that. Because we're all so skeptical, we're all so suspicious. I know I am. It's human nature. But even the skeptics begin to believe in God just because she's so happy with him. And it's not like she's preaching. This woman is just joy and happiness, period.

"She's got ailments and illnesses and has

come near death a couple times, and she is just constantly joyful. I'm happy doing what I'm doing here, but I have bad days. I can't imagine this woman having a bad day. If a wall fell down on her she'd say, 'Isn't that wonderful! Now we can build a new wall.' "

Carroll says poor people thank him. But with Mother Antonia, it's different. "They're thanking me for what I did for them. But with her, there's that sense of happiness just to see her."

Keith MacKay, who works with Carroll, says Mother Antonia's charms have also knocked down bureaucratic obstacles that would have kept donations from reaching the La Mesa prisoners. "We'd go down with truckloads of stuff for her," MacKay says. "And of course at the border the Mexicans stop you going in. But then she would arrive and wave the trucks through. And she'd get away with it. They did anything for Mother Antonia."

Carroll says Mother Antonia's constant sunny demeanor, despite the tragic world where she lives, is hard for some people to understand. "The first time you meet her, you think she's not real. She's nuts, she's not normal," he says. "But in twenty years, I've never seen her change. It's the same exuberance. There's an exuberance about her relationship with God, her relationship with people. Just the joy, the happiness, the love. It is normal. It's what we're supposed to be, and we all wish we could be."

About a year after she had been working in the prison, and had begun working with Jesse and Noreen, word of Mother Antonia's unusual mission had spread throughout Tijuana and San Diego. Many people began calling her the Mother Teresa of Tijuana and the Prison Angel. Father Jaime Rasura, her friend from San Diego who visited her many times, told her the time had come to ask that her work be officially sanctioned by the church, saying, "I love the work you are doing, and I believe that you are Sister Antonia. But we have to have the bishop believe it, too."

Mother Antonia had thought that if she just showed up in Tijuana, worked hard, and kept a low profile, she'd establish a record of good service and eventually might be able to persuade the church authorities to formally accept her. But when Father Rasura advised her to seek the bishop's support right away, she decided he was right. The time had come to face the church.

There were two bishops in the area, Bishop Juan Jesús Posadas Ocampo of

Tijuana and Bishop Leo T. Maher of San Diego, and she felt she should seek the good graces of both. Although her mission centered on the prison in Mexico, she was a U.S. citizen and she frequently crossed into San Diego to seek donations. Father Rasura offered to go with her to see the bishops to help plead her case. But she turned him down because, "If you really believe with all your heart that God is with you, then who else do you need?"

She got on her knees just to make the call to Bishop Posadas's office to ask for an appointment. On the day of their meeting, she went to his office in her homemade habit and knelt before him, asking for his blessing. They sat together and talked for an hour, and she told him her life story, about her two marriages that ended in divorce, her children, everything. Posadas said he admired her work, and that, of course, he would give her his official blessing. He also asked her to take the white habit of the Mercedarians, an eight-hundred-year-old order of priests who had a special devotion to prisoners, and he said he wanted to put the habit on her himself. He would come to the prison to say Mass on September 24, 1978, the feast of Our Lady of Mercy, which commemorates the founding of the Mercedarian order. That would be his last Mass in Tijuana before moving to his new post in Guadalajara, he said; he had been elevated to archbishop. (Posadas, who later became a cardinal, was shot to death in May 1993 as he sat in his car in the Guadalajara airport. Mexican authorities believe he was killed accidentally by assassins from the Arellano Félix drug cartel who were trying to murder a rival drug lord. Posadas's death shocked Mexicans and remains one of the most notorious episodes in recent Mexican history.)

Posadas came and said Mass in the prison's central courtyard. A female prisoner had sewn a new white habit for Mother Antonia. Standing before the bishop in the blazing September heat, Mother Antonia felt a deep satisfaction as he slipped the loose outer part of her white habit over her head and blessed her. For the first time, she felt truly accepted by the church.

The next step was to seek the blessing of Bishop Maher in San Diego. On the day of her appointment with him, when she walked into his big, imposing office, he greeted her with both of his hands held out to her and a warm smile on his face.

"Sister Antonia, I've been waiting for you," he said.

She told him her story, keeping no secrets, and when she finished she looked into his eyes for an answer.

Maher took her hands in his.

"What I want to know, Sister Antonia, is what can I do for you?" he said. "How can I serve you?"

"Your blessing and approval would be wonderful," she replied.

Maher made the decision on the spot to appoint her an auxiliary to the bishop, essentially installing her in an order that reports directly to him. Knowing that there would be some who would object to a twice-divorced mother of seven being a Catholic sister, he told her to send the doubters to him. "I am making you my auxiliary," he said, "and if anybody has any questions, tell them to talk to me."

Carroll says Maher's decision to accept Mother Antonia was entirely in keeping with his personality. "He was the last of the cowboys," he recalls. "He took risks. This wealthy woman comes in and says, 'I wanna be a nun.' Most guys would say, 'Can you call a psychiatrist or something?' But Maher took her vow and let her do her thing. She wasn't asking for anything but permission to give her life to God, and to do it through service to the poor in

Mexico. She did it the right way, but it's a way that most bishops in the modern church would never allow."

She drove back to La Mesa with another unconventional idea in her head: She needed a few good dentists.

SIX

NEW FACES, NEW LIVES

People in Beverly Hills took their smiles for granted. If they didn't have good teeth, they had enough money to get them fixed. But that's not how it was in La Mesa, where many of the prisoners had grown up without running water, let alone toothbrushes. In the poor communities where they came from, every little shop stocked Coke and chocolate bars but rarely toothpaste, and dentists were a distant luxury. So the prison yard was filled with toothless smiles, which Mother Antonia saw as a problem far more serious than simple cosmetics.

"All you have to do is go to a mirror and blacken your front teeth and smile," she says. "It completely changes your appearance. Do you know how hard it is to get a job when you don't have teeth? Your teeth don't say who you are inside, but they are what people judge you by."

Bad teeth certainly weren't the biggest

problem many inmates had, but it was one Mother Antonia knew she could fix. People who like what they see in the mirror feel good about themselves. A few bridges here and a few caps there, and maybe La Mesa would be a better place.

In her first years in the prison, there was a dentist on call to handle emergencies, but she wanted someone to do more than that, to plant teeth where there were none. She first enlisted the help of a couple of prisoners who also happened to be dentists, then she took her campaign to Berlio X. Torres. He was well known in Tijuana as the burly dentist who thundered around on a big Harley-Davidson Chopper, passing out business cards that read, "Ride safely and keep smiling." She persuaded Torres to set up a little office inside La Mesa, and he moved in a chair, an X-ray machine, and a couple of assistants. Mother Antonia started bringing him patients and paying their fees.

Torres had never seen teeth as bad as those he saw in La Mesa. Sometimes he would have a patient with teeth growing sideways, and he would take an impression and study it for days to figure out what to do. "This stuff wasn't in any of my books," he says. He noticed that the worst problems often belonged to the toughest men and women in the prison, and even the hardest cases cried when he showed them their new teeth in the mirror.

Some of the inmates he worked on still stay in touch with him. "They call me all the time and tell me, 'Hey, I'm working over here, I'm working over there,'" he says. "The jobs are no big deal, but they're working, which they couldn't do before, because people didn't accept them. Nobody except Mother Antonia cared for them."

Torres was an early draftee in Mother Antonia's small army of dentists, who donate their labor while she pays laboratory costs, which typically run about two hundred fifty dollars per patient. Another was Humberto Gurmilán, who met Mother Antonia in church. Soon poor patients began showing up at his office, saying simply, "Mother Antonia sent me." One was a young man who had been cleaning windshields on a street corner when Mother Antonia drove up and saw that he was missing his front teeth. She scribbled Gurmilán's name and address on a piece of paper and told him to go see him. The skeptical young man showed up, and Gurmilán fitted him with a new set of front teeth.

Mother Antonia has paid for more than four thousand new smiles.

Once her teeth-fixing operation was under way, she set her sights on facial deformities and scars and the tattoos that marked so many prisoners as gang members or hoodlums. For those, she was going to need a plastic surgeon.

Mother Antonia met Dr. R. Merrel Olesen and his wife, Marie, in 1981 at the home of a mutual friend in San Diego. "In the middle of the party, I came up and found my husband standing there, looking sort of sheepish, with Sister Antonia, who had big tears rolling down her cheeks," Marie recalls. "She said, 'I have been praying for a plastic surgeon to come and help me in my work, and here he is.'"

Merrel, then head of the plastic surgery division at the world-renowned Scripps Clinic and Research Foundation in La Jolla, listened to Mother Antonia's passionate account of how many of the La Mesa inmates, and the guards, could not bear to look at themselves in the mirror because they had horrible birthmarks, scars, and other disfiguring marks. Others had tattoos on their faces, necks, or arms, which marked them as delinquents. All those problems kept them down, kept them from getting a decent job, kept them in crime. Mother Antonia told the Olesens, who had been married only a few weeks, that there were people just across the border who needed them. She hugged them and asked them to please think about helping.

Merrel was deeply moved by Mother Antonia, especially because he knew she had given up a life much like his own, and that she had walked away from wealth and comfort to help the poor in a place he could hardly imagine.

The Olesens got into their car, and Merrel turned to Marie.

"There's one thing you must understand," he said. "There is nothing that lady ever asks of me that I will refuse."

"If that's your other woman," she said, "I have no problem."

A few weeks later, Merrel scrubbed up as best he could in the La Mesa prison infirmary, a modest little room that had been given an extra mopping for the American surgeon's visit. With Marie as his nurse, he laid out a twenty-five-year-old man named César on an ancient gynecological exam table. The young man had a severe and disfiguring cleft lip, a condition Merrel had seen in an adult only once before. In the

United States, cleft lips are routinely fixed in children. But in poor parts of Mexico, they are often left unrepaired.

Merrel arranged the weak lights overhead, the best the prison had to offer. With local anesthetic and surgical tools borrowed from Scripps, the $1,500-an-hour surgeon set to work on the young man's face.

As he worked, Mother Antonia held César's hand.

Not long after the surgery, César's mother came to visit him in the prison.

"Where is César?" she asked Mother Antonia, who was standing right beside her son.

"Mamá, *soy yo,*" César said. "It's me."

The woman started crying when she realized the young man with the normal face was her son.

Over the next nine years, throughout the 1980s, Merrel performed nearly a thousand surgeries, free of charge, in La Mesa. He and Marie made nearly monthly trips to La Mesa, with anesthetic, sutures, and other medicines donated by Scripps and medical supply companies. They operated on eight or ten people on each visit, erasing congenital or acquired deformities, while Mother Antonia held the patients' hands. The table was the wrong height and the conditions were primitive, but Merrel removed glass lodged under the skin from long-ago bar fights and erased hundreds of tattoos, from swastikas to snakes.

Merrel concentrated on facial problems, because Mother Antonia said she wanted the men and women to see someone different when they looked in the mirror. Marie thought that Mother Antonia's reasoning was ahead of her time. "She understood, before it was well recognized, that making physical changes would alter their perceptions of themselves," Marie says. "It wasn't just taking a tattoo off, it was a symbolic transformation enabling them to go forward. I remember thinking how remarkable it was that a religious person saw something so temporal as our appearance as so important."

One of the Olesens' first patients was a young woman known as Licha, short for Alicia, who had tattoos on her face and hands and a long scar across her forehead. The girl had attempted suicide several times. Merrel cut out the tattoos and smoothed out the scar. A week later, on Mexico's Independence Day, the last of the stitches came out. For the first time, Licha walked around the prison yard with her head held high. She told Mother Antonia she wanted to study to be a nurse when she got out of prison.

A few months later, Mother Antonia brought a thirteen-year-old girl named María Lourdes Quintana to see Merrel. María, the daughter of a La Mesa inmate, had fallen from a second-floor window at her home in Tijuana when she was four, smashing her jaw. The damage was not properly treated, and Merrel said part of her jaw essentially fused to her skull. For nine years, she had been eating only what could be sucked through a straw. Her facial muscles had atrophied badly, her jaw had developed much more on one side than the other.

Merrel brought the girl to an oral surgeon friend, Ronald Hecker, who agreed to donate his services and join Merrel in the operation on María. Scripps Memorial Hospital allowed them to perform the surgery there free of cost. Photos from a hospital newsletter at the time show María, a striking beauty even with the jaw problem, sitting in an examining chair with Mother Antonia holding her hands. María went on to become an actress, and she had small parts in several movies.

The Olesens live in an airy home on a hill overlooking the affluent seaside community of La Jolla, in a home decorated with lovely Asian antiques. Merrel, a white-haired man with a surgeon's distinguished carriage and Marcus Welby's gentle face, is not Catholic and said he helped Mother Antonia because she is inspiring and because there was great satisfaction in making such a difference in so many lives. The Olesens learned a few things along the way, too.

Their first trips from La Jolla to La Mesa, in their BMW, were an eye-opening exposure to poverty. As they came to know more inmates, their ideas about the kind of people who are in prison changed, too. Mother Antonia introduced them to Natasha, an English woman who had been sent to prison with her husband, Stewart, for trying to smuggle drugs through Tijuana. "Natasha probably had an IQ of a hundred eighty," Merrel says. "We used to play Scrabble with her, and she beat us by a hundred points every time." When Stewart and Natasha were released from La Mesa, they went to live with the Olesens for a couple of months before they returned to England. The Olesens still get Christmas cards from the couple, who now have two sons.

As the Olesens spent more time with

Mother Antonia, they were struck by how she could be so upbeat in a place of such obvious pain. On a tour of the prison, they came across two inmates playing guitar, and pretty soon Mother Antonia was clapping along to the music. Merrel says there was always someone playing soccer in the yard, and he saw Mother Antonia jump in and kick the ball as they walked past. She was fun, full of life, and fearless.

Merrel and Marie arrived one day just after someone had been murdered, and La Mesa, scary at the best of times, was extremely tense. Any normal person would have wanted to get away for a couple of days to let things calm down, he says, so he asked Mother Antonia to at least come out to dinner with them for a few hours.

"Oh, absolutely not. I can't leave," she said. "Things are so bad here, I need to stay."

Merrel and Marie stopped their monthly prison visits in 1990, after almost a decade, because, they say, "we just ran out of gas." But they still help Mother Antonia with surgical care when she brings patients to the United States and make regular financial contributions to her work, which they consider the labor of a "living saint." These days Mother Antonia often leaves messages on their answering machines, just to let them know that she's thinking of them. Marie always saves the messages, and when she's feeling down, she'll hit the PLAY button to listen to Mother Antonia's bubbly voice, saying something like "Oh, darling, I love you. You're so wonderful."

"She just makes you feel good about yourself," Marie says.

Joanie Kenesie recalls the morning she and Mother Antonia stopped at the Pan Don Pedro bakery to buy bread for the prisoners. Joanie thought the woman behind the counter seemed unfriendly because she hardly smiled and barely made eye contact with them.

When they left the bakery, Mother Antonia looked at Joanie and said, "What a shame about her teeth." Joanie hadn't noticed, but Mother Antonia saw that the woman was missing one of her front teeth. She wasn't unfriendly; she was just embarrassed.

Mother Antonia walked back into the bakery. She took down the woman's name, Leticia López, and her phone number and gave her a piece of paper with Dr. Gurmilán's name and number. She told her to call him to make an appointment to have her teeth fixed.

Leticia couldn't believe a total stranger would do something so kind. She figured it must be some kind of joke, so she didn't bother making the call. Then two weeks later, Carlos Bustamante, who does many errands for Mother Antonia, came into the bakery. "I'm looking for Leticia López," he said, handing her another paper with the dentist's name and number. "Mother Antonia wants to know why you haven't called the dentist. She wants you to make an appointment right away."

Leticia was shocked that Mother Antonia was so interested in helping someone she had met by chance, and that she had actually followed up. She went to see Gurmilán, who ushered her into an examining chair in his small office in a Tijuana strip mall. Before Leticia knew it, the dentist was working on her, and he told her he would have to remove three other damaged teeth and put in a bridge. She was getting nervous because he hadn't said how much all that dental work would cost, and Leticia was pretty much broke.

"He had his hands in my mouth so I couldn't ask him what it was going to cost me," she says.

Leticia had lost her front tooth years earlier when one untreated cavity led to another and the tooth simply fell out. She and her husband already had two teenagers, and she was pregnant again at forty-three. They barely had enough money to feed the kids, so fixing Leticia's smile was a luxury that was out of the question.

"I felt terrible because if I laughed people would turn away," she says. "I could see them looking at my missing tooth. I would look down and try not to smile so they wouldn't see. My husband said it didn't matter, that he loved me like that. But I felt bad and I wanted to be able to smile for him."

When Gurmilán finished working on her teeth that first day, Leticia said, "But doctor, you haven't told me how I'm going to pay you. How much is this going to cost?"

"There is no charge for Mother Antonia's patients," he said.

Several visits later, Leticia walked out of Gurmilán's office with a brand-new porcelain bridge and front teeth.

"I still can't believe it," Leticia says. "There are so many people who need something, so how was she sent to me? I asked God many times to be able to fix my teeth, but we couldn't afford it. Then she just came to me from Heaven."

Leticia now smiles and laughs so much that people tell her she's a flirt. But she says she just likes to talk to everyone because she feels so good.

"My husband asks me if I'm ever going to stop smiling," she says. "And I say, 'never.'"

SEVEN

ALIAS *"LA SISTER"*

Mother Antonia had heard about the *Grito,* the cry, from one prisoner after another. It was an initiation rite that prisoners feared, and everyone had a story about it, including Guadalupe Arroyo, a thirty-two-year-old mother who had been arrested on a marijuana-possession charge.

On her first morning in La Mesa, seventy guards were crammed into a long, narrow passageway that had no roof and felt cold as a tomb. Guards in black leather jackets and warm boots lined each side, their backs against the dull beige walls. In the small space of the hallway, they could reach across and touch each other. They joked and smoked and laughed, keys and nightsticks hanging from their belts.

Time to start.

They all turned their heads toward the end of the corridor, where Guadalupe — known as Lupe — stood shivering.

151

She stood there in a thin blouse and pants, nauseated. The mother of two small children, who was expecting her third, had been arrested when police stopped her car and found some marijuana. They accused her of being a major drug dealer and turned her over to the federal police. She said she had no idea the pot was in the car, and later figured that a friend must have put it there, knowing that she frequently drove from Tijuana across the border into San Diego, where she now lived. But the cops at the police station weren't buying her story and decided they would beat the truth out of her. They put plastic bags over her head to make her think she would suffocate, slapped her around, and kicked her. When she still wouldn't confess, they sent her to La Ocho, a city jail named for its location on Eighth Street, to await trial. Then, without warning, she was transferred to La Mesa.

Now, on her first morning in the state penitentiary, she and ten other new prisoners stood at the end of a hallway filled with the stale smell of sweat. She shook from cold and fear. What did these guards want? More plastic bags? More beatings? Worse? What did they do to women in this place?

Then suddenly she felt the presence of

something warm. She saw a small woman in a white habit speaking Spanish but obviously not Mexican, walking along the line, pressing bars of soap, toilet paper, and toothbrushes into the trembling hands of the new prisoners. Lupe couldn't take her eyes off Mother Antonia.

A guard yelled to the newcomers, "This is the *Grito*. You will stand up straight. You will walk down this hallway. You will shout out your name, your alias, and the charge against you. You will yell loud, and you will yell clear. You will do it three times. You will do it right, or you will be sorry."

Three men standing in front of Lupe went first, one by one. They shuffled because the police had taken their shoelaces, and some held their pants up with their hands because the police had taken their belts. They shouted their names and nicknames. One was *El Diablo,* another *El Chupacabras,* the Devil and the Goat Sucker. Those names sounded cool on the street, but the guards howled with laughter. The men walked through the narrow gauntlet with the guards yelling at them just inches from their faces.

Lupe took a deep breath. She started walking.

"Guadalupe Arroyo! Drugs!"

"What's your alias?"

"I don't have one."

"What kind of drugs?"

"Marijuana!"

"Say it again!"

Her breath came fast and shallow. She struggled to shout loud.

"Guadalupe Arroyo! Marijuana!"

The guards yelled at her. "Keep walking straight! Yell it louder!" She kept her head up and tried to stare off into nowhere, being sure to avoid eye contact, the way you do with a dog baring its teeth. Her stomach heaved, and she wanted to throw up, sick that the baby inside her had to go through this. She raged silently that she had to yell out a crime she didn't commit.

"Guadalupe Arroyo! Marijuana!"

At last, she reached the end of the long prison passageway and arrived at the main yard. She had survived her first *Grito*. The head guard told the prisoners they would do the same thing again the next two mornings at seven o'clock. Every new prisoner went through the *Grito* three times, so that all three shifts of guards could have a look at them and so every prisoner would know who was boss.

The next morning Lupe looked for Mother Antonia as she lined up for the

Grito. But she wasn't there, and these guards were different, harsher. One man didn't shout his name loud enough, and the guards smacked him on the head. They punched another man on his neck and back. Lupe tried to do everything right, but they still pushed her. That day the *Grito* wasn't only about humiliation, it was also about pain. Lupe fought back the tears and thought, *I have to find that nun or I won't be able to bear this place.*

Mother Antonia had complained about the *Grito* from the minute she first heard about it. She thought it stripped the prisoners — many of whom were simply awaiting trial and had not even been convicted of any crime — of their last shreds of dignity. It also perpetuated La Mesa's culture of violence, where disputes were sometimes settled in the prison yard with knives, pistols, and even, on occasion, Uzis. On a single day in 1978, eight people, including the warden, were killed during a fierce shootout in the prison yard. There was violence between prisoners, among gangs, and by guards who thought nothing of maintaining order at the end of a nightstick or with their steel-toed boots.

She asked the warden many times to

155

eliminate the *Grito,* but the answer never changed: It helped maintain discipline, and guards needed to know every prisoner's name and the crime they committed. She asked the comandante, the head of the guards, over and over again for permission to attend the *Grito,* but it was four years before he agreed. In the meantime, she began her quiet crusade to stop the abuse of prisoners by talking to the guards one at a time.

She asked them to put themselves in the prisoners' shoes. She reminded them how they were coming from police custody, where many of them had been beaten and tortured. She told them the prisoners had not had a bath in days, and that they were hungry and scared and alone.

"How would you like to have to yell out 'For Rape! For Rape! For Rape!' And what if you were innocent?" she told the guards. They had no right to appoint themselves judges. Even if the prisoners were guilty, she told them, "We are not our mistakes and our errors. Nobody in the world would want the worst thing they ever did stamped on their forehead."

Whenever she could, she gave prisoners a cool cloth to wash their faces or a comb to brush their hair in front of the guards. She thought if they saw her caring for the prisoners and treating them with respect, the guards would be less likely to degrade them.

Mother Antonia came to realize that much of the problem was that the guards had little or no training. They also worked twenty-four-hour shifts and were often exhausted from long nights standing on the wall. Some took speed or other drugs to stay awake all night, and that made them more aggressive toward the prisoners. Mother Antonia made regular late-night visits to guards standing in the cold on the walls, bringing them hot towels to wrap their legs and ease their cramps, and pots of hot chocolate to warm them. Playing Ping-Pong with them on their breaks in the middle of the night, she never stopped telling them that judges, not guards, decide guilt or innocence and that no one deserves to be slapped or kicked or beaten.

When Mother Antonia saw a guard or a police officer roughing up a prisoner, she often reminded them, "Don't forget, that is Christ you have in your hands."

Once a *federale,* a member of the federal judicial police, shouted back at her, "*Madre,* is Christ a drug trafficker?"

"Yes," she said. "And he is a *federale,* too."

For every hour she spent with a sick inmate in the infirmary, she spent another with the guards, staying up with them, learning the names of their wives and girlfriends and children. Sometimes she paid medical bills for their children, as she did for the prisoners, and she sympathized with how hard it was to do such a difficult job for so little pay. Many of them had never considered many of the things she talked about, like basic human rights.

The guards learned to give her space to work. Anthony Solano, the prison administrator, says it was sometimes difficult for guards to see Mother Antonia hug men who had been convicted of rape or murder. But they learned to respect how she saw only the best in everyone, including them. He recalls a day when she drove up in her car, full of used clothes, carpets, and other goods, and the guards grabbed everything for themselves. "I was angry, and she was sad," Solano says. "Those things were for the prisoners. But she just said, 'The guards need things, too. Look at how little they get paid.'"

Apolinar Aguilar Nieto, who met Mother Antonia as a prison guard in the 1970s, says guards respect her constant insistence on decent treatment for prisoners and marvel at how she takes risks that even guards wearing bulletproof vests would not. He recalls the night a large group of inmates got drunk on homemade grain alcohol in celebration of Mexican Independence Day. One thing led to another, and suddenly they were stealing food out of the prison kitchen and starting fires and smashing shops in *El Pueblito.* Aguilar watched as Mother Antonia stepped in to talk to the rioting inmates, acting as a liaison between them and the guards. "She risked her life for all of us," says Aguilar, who later became head of the guards. "Once you see her in action, you know she is one in a million."

Mother Antonia also brought her message of nonviolence to police stations. She told the officers, who often interrogated suspects with their fists, that in the end, the torturer suffers more than the victim. So many wives and girlfriends have told her how torturers scream out in the middle of the night, haunted by what they have done.

She wrote a "Prayer for Police," which she passed out to officers and which hangs in police stations all over Baja California. "Help me remember that there is no justice without mercy," it reads. "Give me compassion that I may have compassion for those who need it."

Over the years, Tijuana police officers started calling her on her cell phone, asking her to come to the scene when an officer was injured or killed. Increasingly, the officers have sought out her comfort and help.

In 1996, as she attended the funeral of yet another slain officer, she thought of another way to help them. As she heard the police choir singing on the altar, she realized that if they recorded a tape or CD, she could help them sell it. There was no pension for Tijuana police, so when an officer died, his widow often had no means of support. That was the beginning of *Brazos Abiertos,* Open Arms, a charity dedicated to the widows and orphans of Tijuana police officers, which raises thousands of dollars a year. Mother Antonia raises some of it herself, sometimes standing at busy downtown intersections with a cup for donations. Once she auctioned off a pair of donated diamond earrings for ten thousand dollars — more than a year's salary for most police officers. When the city created its first nursery school specifically for the children of police, they named it for Mother Antonia.

Inside La Mesa, she began winning the battle against the *Grito* on her fourth anniversary, in 1981, when she again asked the head of guards for permission to attend and again was denied.

"But it's my anniversary!" she pleaded.

Her anniversary had become an important date in the prison, and every year the guards gave her a cake. She stood before the comandante, holding her cake and giving him a look that he couldn't resist. Melting, he said, "Okay, Okay."

The next morning, Mother Antonia took her place alongside the prisoners at the *Grito*. A guard who had been particularly friendly with Mother Antonia was so shocked when he saw her in line with the ragged newcomers that he literally almost fainted; for a second he thought she had been arrested. Mother Antonia moved among the new prisoners, explaining the process to them. "Do exactly as the guards tell you, stand up straight, yell out clearly. This, too, will pass," she told them. The guards yelled, but they didn't lay a hand on anyone.

The following day she showed up again, but the comandante called her back: "I said you could go yesterday for your anniversary."

"Oh, Comandante, you didn't say I could go just one day! It was my present that I could attend the *Grito* from now on!"

The comandante realized he had been checkmated. Smiling, he gave in, but added one condition. If Mother Antonia wanted to attend, she had to participate. She loved the idea. She strode into the hallway, right past the new prisoners huddled against the cold. In her habit — clean, pressed, and snow white — she headed down the line. She marched straight like a soldier, remembering the military skills she learned in the volunteer ambulance corps on the streets of Beverly Hills. At the end of the line, she did a crisp about-face and returned, calling out her name and alias three times:

"Mother Antonia Brenner Clarke!

"Alias: *La Sister!*"

The amused guards yelled out: "Why are you here?"

"For the love of God and for the love of you all!"

The *Grito* became a crucial part of her daily routine: up before dawn, prayers in the chapel, then the *Grito,* unless some emergency kept her away. She brought baby wipes to wash prisoners' faces. She handed out shirts and socks and food to those who had none. She passed out soaps and shampoos from nice hotels in California that her friends had collected. Many of the prisoners didn't know how to read the hotel names stamped on the bars of soap, but their sweet smell was often the first pleasant thing that had come their way in a long time.

She took to imitating the walk of the *cholos,* the Mexican youths who had lived in the United States and who all seemed to have perfected the same slouching gait. Everyone laughed, but she had a point: Don't walk like a hoodlum, and you won't be treated like a hoodlum. Stand up straight and proud, because "People can take your life without your permission, but they can't take your dignity unless you give it to them."

One day she brought a cassette player to the *Grito*. She played love songs by Julio Iglesias and Pedro Infante, the beloved old-time Mexican movie star and singer. The cold tension in the atmosphere melted immediately, like an ice cube dropped into a cup of steaming tea. She asked everyone to forget where they were for a moment. Think of something beautiful in your life, she said, let your mind wander back to a time when you felt most loved. As the sweet melody played on, some guards and prisoners turned their faces to the wall so no one would see the tears in their eyes. Others lowered their heads. Every one of them had been in love, and Mother Antonia had brought that back to them. Love songs became a new regular feature of the *Grito*.

The *Grito* always followed the six o'clock List, the daily prisoner roll call. The count was to be sure nobody had escaped overnight. But it served another purpose when guards wanted to make a little money. They would sometimes charge prisoners a fifty-cent fee to mark them present, which added up when paid by thousands of inmates every day. Prisoners knew that if they weren't checked in by the guards, they wouldn't get credit for serving that day of their sentence, which meant they would have to stay in prison longer. So they paid, even if it meant having no money to eat that day.

One morning a new young prisoner, dreading the coming *Grito,* hid from the guards and missed the count. The guards fumed. They were finishing a dreary twenty-four-hour shift and could not go home until all prisoners were accounted for. Hunting angrily for the young man, they eventually dragged him out of his hiding place, barefoot and crying. Mother Antonia followed them, worried about what was coming. A big guard smashed the young man with his fist. As he raised his hand to hit him a second time, Mother Antonia screamed: "Take your hands off him!" But the guard hit him again anyway, and she started to cry. The other guards were amazed that he had hit a prisoner in front of Mother Antonia. She was so angered by the incident that she didn't want to attend the *Grito* that was about to start. But she made herself go anyway.

That morning, she called out her name in a defiant voice.

A guard who saw the anger flaring in her eyes asked her what was wrong.

"In English, 'coward' is the word we use for hitting defenseless people," she yelled. "But if you have a better word in Spanish, tell me."

No one spoke.

After she attended the *Grito* every morning for more than a decade, a high-ranking soldier in the Mexican army, Major Miguel Angel Pérez, took over as warden. As she had with a long line of new directors, Mother Antonia introduced herself and told him that the first thing he should do was cancel the *Grito*. He had never heard of it, and when she explained it to him, he said it sounded ridiculous and unprofessional. He immediately ordered changes. No more

165

forcing prisoners to yell out their crimes. No more walking the gauntlet between the rows of guards. From now on, they would simply stand in front of the guards and call out their name and aliases. He reasoned that the guards needed to know the prisoners' names, but they didn't need to humiliate them, and the guards, after years of Mother Antonia's presence at the *Grito,* took it in stride. They even joked with her in the *Grito:* "We can't hear you! Shout it louder!" To their delight, she repeated "Alias: *La Sister!*" over and over.

At last, one morning she saw her years of quiet work pay off. A new prisoner at the *Grito* was too weak or too scared to shout out his name in front of everyone. Rather than abusing him, a guard spoke up for the inmate and shouted his name for him.

"After so many years, her work is bearing fruit," says La Mesa prison guard Pablo Lamegos Méndez. He says for years and years she has been telling guards that the prisoners "are here for making a mistake, that we shouldn't hit them," and her work has paid off. "The guards don't touch the prisoners anymore. Nowadays I don't see guards hitting prisoners, even when she is not there."

In August 2003, the *Grito* was eliminated entirely.

Mary Clarke at about age fifteen, serving in the volunteer ambulance corps during World War II.

Mary with her sixth child, Thomas, in 1955.

The Brenner family in 1956.

Monsignor Anthony Brouwers, Mother Antonia's namesake, on the right, with Bishop Timothy Manning.

Mother Antonia in her cell, 1980.

Guards line up atop La Mesa Prison, 2003.

Archie Moore, the boxer, on his visit to La Mesa in 1981.

A birthday celebration outside Mother Antonia's cell, 1982.

Mother Antonia in 1979, with a group of prison guards in La Mesa.

Instructions Mother Antonia posted to explain the *Grito* to new prisoners.

Mother Antonia with Rigoberto Campos Salcido, Rigo. This photo hangs in a frame on a wall at Casa Campos de San Miguel.

Viviana and Mario, the children who survived the Ensenada massacre, at the military hospital in Ensenada.

Mother Antonia
with Robert
Hernandez,
2004.

Mother Antonia meets Pope John Paul II on
Mother's Day at an outdoor Mass in
Chihuahua City, Mexico, 1990.
(Courtesy of Archbishop Emilio Carlos Berlie)

Mother Antonia in 1987, in her 1979 Checker Cab, a twelve-seater that she packed full of donations to take to the prison.
(Courtesy of Olivia Fregoso)

Mother Antonia at a celebration to honor the Tijuana police force. The caption read, "Behave well, young man." (Courtesy of Sergio Ortiz, *La Frontera*)

Mother Antonia and her fellow sisters in the Servants of the Eleventh Hour, at Casa Campos de San Miguel.

Thanksgiving photo of Mother Antonia's family, 2004. (Courtesy of William Avnon)

EIGHT

SEEKING JUSTICE

The more inmates Mother Antonia met, the more she was struck by how many of them didn't deserve to be locked up. She often meets people who believe that everyone in prison probably deserves to be there, but in La Mesa she discovered that is anything but the truth.

She found the prison was choked with inmates who had committed the slightest of crimes, many of whom had stolen food to eat. She met some serving long sentences for stealing a jacket or a pair of shoes. Many were simply awaiting trial and didn't have bail money, and hundreds more had been convicted of misdemeanors and ordered to pay as little as a twenty-five-dollar fine in lieu of jail. They didn't have the money, so they had to do the time. Others were lost in the system, stuck in prison beyond their release dates because of abysmal record-keeping or other administrative blunders. A Guatemalan house painter spent more than a year in La Mesa because police were sure he was a Mexican man wanted for robbery. A sympathetic human rights group finally proved that he was the wrong man — their photos looked nothing alike — and he went free after losing fifteen months of his life.

The Mexican justice system, like many around the world, is stacked against the poor. The wealthy use high-priced lawyers and political connections to stay out of prison, while poor people who commit petty crimes are locked up. Bankers and politicians who have embezzled millions walk around free, but the system comes down like a sledgehammer on minor offenders. We have come across many such cases, including a man sentenced to three years for stealing a Gansito, a sweet roll like a Twinkie, and another who served six years for stealing bread. A college student who used a fake ID to get on the Mexico City subway, instead of paying the twenty-cent fare, served two months in prison and paid a fifteen-hundred-dollar fine. Poorly trained police tend to focus on the easiest crimes to solve, like street robberies, while legislators under political pressure to combat rising crime rates set tough minimum sentences for the smallest of offenses. The inequality reminds Mother Antonia of a quote from Bishop Oscar Romero, a personal hero of hers who was murdered in El Salvador in 1980: "The law is like a serpent. It bites the feet which have no shoes on."

Mother Antonia quickly realized after moving into La Mesa that she could free many prisoners, mainly first offenders convicted of nonviolent crimes, by paying their bails or fines. She looks at a donated hundred-dollar bill and sees four free men. So she started visiting courthouses all over Tijuana and the rest of Baja California state, pleading for mercy and paying the fines of thousands of men and women.

She also started representing prisoners at their court appearances. The first time was to plead the case of a young couple who had been convicted of helping smuggle people across the border into the United States. The couple, who were raising a baby in La Mesa, worked at the prison cleaning and ironing for wealthier prisoners to raise money to pay their fine. They were still about a thousand dollars short when Mother Antonia went to court to plead for their freedom, telling the judge that they had never broken the law before, they were never violent, and they had been exemplary prisoners. The judge waived the rest of their fine, and they were released.

As she became a familiar sight in the courthouses and got to know the judges better, Mother Antonia began raising the issue of the unfairness she saw in sentencing. She repeatedly saw those who killed a wealthy person sentenced to twenty-five years or more, while those who killed a poor person got off with as little as four years.

"Isn't everybody's life just as valuable?" she asked Miguel Angel Barud, a judge in Tijuana.

Barud, who calls Mother Antonia a "refreshing Coca-Cola in the desert," says her persistent arguments changed the way he sentences people and reminded him that a victim's social standing must be irrelevant. "There are fewer and fewer people who worry about others in this world," the judge says. "I wish there were more Mother Antonias."

For Mother Antonia, the injustice of the system was personified by a young man named Arturo, whom she met in 1985, balled up and writhing in agony in the prison infirmary.

She sat next to him on his bed. He said he had been suffering with stomach pain for days before he finally ended up in the infirmary, a dormitory-style room with a couple of windows covered in heavy mesh looking out over the prison yard. Mother Antonia had never seen him before, even though he had been in the prison for several months. He quietly blended in with thousands of other inmates with the same dark skin and hair, another twentysomething face in the crowd. Invisible but everywhere, he was the Everyman of the prison yard.

When Arturo first came in, the prison doctor told him his pain would pass eventually. Probably just a stomach bug. Nothing serious. But after a couple of days of intensifying pain, it became obvious that Arturo had grave problems, and he was finally sent by ambulance to General Hospital, where the city's poor competed for the attention of overwhelmed and undersupplied doctors. Mother Antonia climbed into the ambulance with him, as she so often did with critically ill patients. Arturo grimaced in pain, and she held his hand.

Doctors who met the ambulance were furious. The most cursory examination in the emergency room showed that Arturo had a severe case of appendicitis. He should have been brought in much sooner. The doctors rushed him to surgery. Mother Antonia waited, and when the surgeon finally emerged, he said Arturo's appendix had burst and that the damage and infection were irreversible.

"He's going to die," the doctor snapped, fuming about the medical care Arturo had received at La Mesa. Appendix problems can be difficult to diagnose, he said, but Arturo's problems were like a giant billboard advertising his condition, and the prison doctor should have spotted it. They wheeled Arturo into the intensive care unit, a modest ward with only the basics of medical care. Nurses wandered in and out, doing their best to comfort him, but they had no morphine for his pain. So instead they gave Mother Antonia a towel, which she used to mop up the sweat pouring off him. The infection had spread throughout his body, and he burned with fever. Mother Antonia folded the towel and placed it under his head, then on his face, neck, and chest. She wrung out the towel over and over. Badly dehydrated, Arturo ached with thirst. Mother Antonia soaked a small piece of gauze and pressed it against his dry lips. She knew that only his youth and strength allowed him to bear so much pain for so long.

Over the next few hours, she learned about the young man dying before her. He had come to Tijuana from his home somewhere in the center of the country, hoping to sneak into the United States to find work. Millions of Mexicans pick tomatoes or mow lawns for minimum wage in the United States as a way out of poverty. But Arturo ran out of money as he waited for his chance to cross. So one night, broke and hundreds of miles from home, he and another man robbed someone on the street and stole eight dollars.

"I didn't have a penny, but I was hungry," he told Mother Antonia. "I didn't want to steal."

A police officer saw the robbery and grabbed Arturo, who ended up before a judge a few days later. There had been no weapon involved and no one had been hurt, so the judge ordered Arturo to pay a twenty-five-dollar fine. But he had no money and no friends in Tijuana to help him. He was too ashamed to contact his parents for help, so he went to La Mesa.

As Arturo lay in the hospital bed, Mother Antonia asked him about his family. Who could she call for him? There must be someone worried. A mother? A girlfriend? Someone must be losing sleep at night wondering what had happened to him. But Arturo wouldn't talk about it. He insisted that his family not be told. Mother Antonia figured Arturo probably came from a family that never before had trouble with the law. Even facing death, he seemed willing to simply disappear rather than shame them.

Mother Antonia checked the prison records and found that Arturo had given a fake address and an especially common and almost certainly false last name, like González or Martínez. She never knew his real name. All that was clear was that for lack of twenty-five dollars, Arturo had passed month after month in La Mesa.

In the hospital that night, Mother Antonia held Arturo's hand as midnight came and went. She didn't want him to die alone. She mopped his face and wet his cracked lips with gauze. He kissed her hand and asked if the police were guarding his room, and Mother Antonia told him they were.

"Tell them I didn't want to break the law. God knows I'm sorry, Mother."

"I know He does, Arturo. And He forgives you."

Arturo repeated over and over: "I want to be free. I want to die a free man." Mother Antonia wanted to give him something to hope for, so she told him to hang on until Monday. It was before dawn on Saturday, but if he could make it until Monday morning, she would go see a judge. Surely he would free Arturo.

"Aguanta. Aguanta," she told him. Bear it. Bear it.

"I'm going to bear it, Mother," he said. "I want to be free."

Mother Antonia sat on a chair beside Arturo's bed. He drifted off to sleep sometimes, but the pain kept waking him up. Just before dawn, Arturo opened his eyes and asked Mother Antonia the time. She told him it was five. Alarmed, Arturo said he needed to get to La Mesa to pass the morning List, the six o'clock prisoner roll call. He knew if he didn't, he wouldn't get credit for having served that day.

Mother Antonia knew Arturo couldn't move. She looked at a doctor who had just arrived.

"He's not going to pass List this morning, Mother," he said.

Mother Antonia sat with Arturo and watched him die. He stayed conscious almost to the end. Then he dropped off to sleep around six o'clock, and she watched his heart rate on a monitor fall suddenly. Forty-six, then ten, then zero, zero, zero.

She kissed him on the forehead and held him in her arms, and she blessed him as she made him a promise: "I swear, Arturo, you will not die in vain. I will tell people always how you came here to Tijuana looking for work. How you were an accomplice to an eight-dollar robbery and you died because of it. I will tell people that there are men like you all over the world in prisons. You will not be unknown, Arturo. I'm going to tell everybody. Your life will count."

Arturo's family probably thought he died trying to cross the border or maybe they thought he made it across, started a new life, and forgot them. Mother Antonia was upset that they would never know what happened to him. The only thing she could do for them, and for Arturo, was to give him a decent burial.

The hospital sent Arturo's body to the city morgue, where Mother Antonia knew the routine well. His family had nine days to claim his body. If no one came, he would be buried in an unmarked pauper's grave at Tijuana's New Municipal Cemetery. There are two kinds of burials for the poor there: either in an unmarked common grave or in modest individual plots where a small marker is allowed. The second type is only slightly more dignified, a temporary upgrade on the passage to the beyond. After five years, those caskets are moved to common graves to make way for others. It is where Mother Antonia wants to be buried, among her *hijos,* in a space that can eventually be given to someone else.

When no one claimed Arturo's body, Mother Antonia bought a pine coffin for him and paid the small fee to bury it. She marked his grave with a small wooden cross. As they lowered him into the grave, nuns and grave diggers bowed their heads and said a prayer for a man they had never met.

The next week Mother Antonia took her anger and sadness about Arturo's death to the Tijuana courthouses. She went to judge after judge and told them the story. They seemed genuinely disgusted. Several promised to review their files for others stuck in prison for minor offenses. Within a week, she and the judges arranged for seventy-five men to be freed.

Mother Antonia knows that the country's prisons are still overflowing with poor people who committed petty offenses. But she keeps trying to get them out. In all of them, she sees Arturo.

"To me Arturo is the Unknown Prisoner," she says. "You can multiply him by thousands all over the world. They were hungry, and they took something to eat. Or they couldn't find a job and they were desperate, and they took something that didn't add up to ten dollars. Then they came to prisons and died and were buried, and nobody knows that they ever lived."

Mother Antonia's initial focus had been on the immediate and practical needs of prisoners, like bread or eyeglasses or medicine. But as she witnessed so many cases of injustice, she began pressing for more fundamental changes to the torture, abuse, and inequality of the Mexican justice system. She knew there were many human rights leaders agitating on the outside, marching and carrying signs. She always thought she could do the most good on the inside.

She had to be careful about how hard she pushed. Several times she could easily have blown the whistle on some particular guard or police officer for abusing prisoners. But she didn't see what good that would do. First, the federal, state, and local authorities all used the same bare-knuckle techniques, so there were few places to complain. Going to the media might have shined a light on the problem, but only a temporary one. A few guards might be fired for damage control, but nothing would really change, and she might cause enough resentment to get herself thrown out of La Mesa. Then thousands of prisoners who depended on her would be the losers. Sometimes, frustrated by the slow pace of change, she thought about quitting and joining a human rights group. But in the end, she always concluded that there were plenty of people on the outside working for justice, but she was the only one on the inside. So she kept trying to quietly change the culture of the place by talking with the guards, police, and judges rather than going public.

Still, there have been times when she felt she had to speak out, no matter what the risks.

The first was the case of Rubén Oropeza Hurtado, a tough guy from the streets of Tijuana, thirty-nine years old with an athlete's trim build. The federal judicial police brought him to La Mesa one night in April 1990. He had been arrested eleven days before, charged with possession of a small amount of marijuana and heroin. The *federales* had been holding him since then in their headquarters, the most feared four walls in the city.

Low-slung and beige, the concrete office building just a few yards south of the U.S. border in downtown Tijuana looked ordinary enough. But when parents, wives, or girlfriends heard that a loved one had been taken inside, they came weeping to the doors, some on their knees in prayer. The federal police, those in charge of investigating all drug crimes in Mexico, routinely extracted confessions and information by beatings and torture, including a favorite technique of placing a plastic bag over a suspect's head and blowing it full of cigarette smoke. Sometimes the interrogators were just hired thugs, not even the police themselves.

For the eleven days Rubén was held there, interrogators repeatedly stomped on his stomach, driving their heavy boots into his guts. They wanted to know the name of his drug supplier. When they had finished, the only facts established beyond doubt were that Rubén was indeed a penny-ante drug dealer, and that his smashed intestines were slowly filling with blood.

When he was moved to La Mesa, he did

not seem critically ill at first. He walked around the prison yard sharing his story with other prisoners who had similar tales of brutality. In those days in Tijuana, as in much of the country, police had little training in even the most basic investigative techniques. Gathering physical evidence to prove a suspect's guilt was nearly unheard of. The standard police procedure was to inflict as much pain as needed until the suspect signed a confession. But in 1990, Mexico had started trying to improve its international reputation. President Carlos Salinas de Gortari had just created a National Human Rights Commission, a move he hoped would bolster Mexico's image abroad and improve the standing of its corrupt and ineffective legal system. The Harvard-educated Salinas was pushing Mexico to join the world economy, and the North American Free Trade Agreement, which took effect in 1994, was in the works. Salinas knew that foreign investors were leery of sinking money into a country with such weak rule of law. The human rights commission was a first step designed to prove that Mexico could act more like a First World country.

Human rights lawyers were suddenly allowed inside La Mesa after years of being locked out, and Rubén and about sixty other prisoners met with Víctor Clark Alfaro, a pioneering human rights defender in Tijuana. The prisoners felt emboldened enough in July 1990 to begin a hunger strike. They carried signs that read ENOUGH TORTURE and marched through the prison yard, demanding a stop to brutal police practices and poor prison conditions. Clark Alfaro, a friend of Mother Antonia, organized victims of police abuse and documented their cases in writing and photos to draw public attention to the problem.

On a Saturday night, July 14, in the middle of the hunger strike, Mother Antonia was called into the infirmary. A prisoner was in critical condition and needed to go immediately to the hospital. Mother Antonia climbed into the back of the ambulance to comfort the man lying on the stretcher. He was in terrible pain. As she smoothed back his hair, she saw that it was Rubén. They had first met when he was in La Mesa years before on a minor marijuana charge. He told her then that he was infuriated that big-time *narcos* paid bribes and went free while police threw the book at little guys like him.

Now Rubén didn't have the strength to

talk. He was too sick. In a prison filled with thousands of inmates, Mother Antonia hadn't realized how ill he had been. Inmates constantly approached her in the prison yard, asking her to buy medicine, to pay for an operation, for a phone call to a relative, for a lawyer — anything. But Rubén never had. It had been three months since the stomping that had left his torso covered with dark purple bruises. Mother Antonia was upset with herself for not recognizing that he was sicker than the others on the hunger strike.

When they arrived at the Red Cross Hospital downtown, doctors and nurses quickly rushed Rubén into surgery. An emergency room examination showed that he was not suffering from his hunger strike, as some prison officials thought, but from infections in his mashed intestines. He had been slowly dying from his injuries for weeks.

Sister Dolores, a nun working in the operating room, watched as surgeons found a collapsed left lung, a herniated diaphragm, and yard after yard of black intestines. They cut it out of him like rotten sausage and dropped it, wet and heavy and dead, into a bucket. Then they sewed up his hollowed-out abdomen. They concluded that he would live for only a matter of weeks, having lost his entire small intestine and 70 percent of his colon. For the rest of what remained of his life, Rubén would have to be fed intravenously.

Sister Dolores was horrified listening to doctors discuss the brutality of the beatings that he had obviously suffered. She came out of the operating room, angry and emotional, and showed Mother Antonia the bucket filled with Rubén's guts. "Why didn't they just take a gun and shoot him?" Then she turned to Mother Antonia and said darkly, "How can you work with men who do this?"

"Because I can help make it better — maybe not all better, but better," Mother Antonia said. It was how she always answered that kind of question. But there were moments, like now, when she wondered. It rang in her ears and drowned out her thoughts: *How can you work with men who do this?*

She went to see the commander of the federal judicial police in Tijuana and confronted him about Rubén's beating. He was a new commander, not the one on the job when Rubén was abused, but she still wanted him to take responsibility for his men.

"It didn't happen here, Mother," he said.

"It *DID, Comandante,*" she insisted.

She looked around the room at other *federales* sitting there. She pointed angrily at their feet. "Do you think God gave you those boots so you could go around kicking people?"

The police all looked at the floor. They said nothing.

A day or two later, investigators from the new human rights commission arrived in Tijuana. They came to La Mesa to have a look at prison conditions, and they sought out Mother Antonia. While they were talking, she received a call from the hospital. Rubén's condition was getting worse, and he might die within hours. She excused herself, telling the investigators that she had to go to the hospital to see one of her *hijos* who was in grave condition.

They asked what happened to him.

Mother Antonia had her chance. She took it. This was the moment to go public.

"It was a police interrogation. He's not going to live," she told them. "Why don't you come see him?"

They arranged to meet at the hospital that night at eleven, after their other meetings were finished. Mother Antonia went to Rubén and explained about the men

193

who were coming from Mexico City. At first he didn't want to talk to them. He worried it was a trick, perhaps they were really police who might kill him right then if he tried to speak out about his torture.

"You have to speak up," Mother Antonia told him. "You can't let this chance go by. Think of the people who will come after you."

Many thousands of men and women had been tortured by Mexican police, but it was rare that anyone spoke out publicly. Many of the victims were dead. Those who survived were too afraid to say anything. Even if they did, the word of a criminal suspect rarely carries weight in Mexican courts. Judges all the way to the Supreme Court have regularly ruled that just because a confession was extracted by torture doesn't necessarily mean it is false.

But this case was different. Rubén was dying. And he had the chance to talk to investigators appointed by the president himself. He agreed to see them, and they came into his hospital room in suits and ties, carrying notebooks.

"Hola amigo," one said. "What happened to you?"

Rubén pulled down the sheet covering him, giving them a long look at the scars.

"My lungs, my guts, my body. They're gone."

"Who did this?"

"The *federales,*" Rubén said.

He described the hours of beating and torture, and the investigators wrote it all down. The interview was brief and powerful.

"It was an important moment in the history of fighting against torture," says Clark Alfaro, who had been pressuring the government to confront the torturers in many cases, including Rubén's. Mother Antonia sees Rubén's case as similar to that of Rodney King, the black man whose beating at the hands of the L.A. police was captured on video, bringing new accountability to law enforcement.

A month after the investigators saw Rubén, on August 29, 1990, the commission issued a report concluding that Rubén had been tortured and recommending that two federal judicial police officers be suspended and punished. It was official — in black and white, a government-sanctioned commission said government-paid officers had abused their authority and mortally wounded a petty drug pusher. It was one of the commission's first major actions. Rubén's case had become a rallying point, and prisoners in La Mesa who had formed their own human rights group named it after him.

Still, change wasn't going to be that easy. Faced with the commission's findings, the federal attorney general's office began covering up fast. It released its own report on Rubén's case, taking exception to the commission's findings and laying out its own memorable version of the facts. Rubén had pulverized all his own internal organs, the attorney general said, by "hitting himself against a car" while crazed on drugs. In the end, no one was ever punished. The human rights community was disappointed, but not surprised.

Despite the official stonewalling in Rubén's case, Mother Antonia has seen a radical improvement in the treatment of prisoners over the years, and she believes Rubén's case helped lead the way.

In the last days of Rubén's life, in September 1990, his girlfriend, Paty, gave birth to their second child, a baby boy they named Rubén. Mother Antonia called Bishop Berlie, who presided over a remarkable ceremony at Rubén's bedside, where he baptized the baby and at the same time married Rubén and Paty. Berlie's presence was a public symbol. Bishops usually don't baptize babies for men in prison. But Mother Antonia persuaded him to use Rubén's case as a way for the church to publicly press for more humane treatment of prisoners.

Newspaper and television cameras were called in to record it all. Mother Antonia stood next to Rubén's bed, telling reporters with the cameras rolling, "Stop the torture. Stop the torture. Stop the torture."

Headlines the next day read, THE CHURCH SPEAKS.

NINE

HUMAN BEINGS LIKE ANYONE ELSE

Mother Antonia's adopted home is a major crossroads of drug trafficking. Perhaps no city along the two-thousand-mile U.S.–Mexico border has had more drug smuggling and violence than Tijuana, which always seems to give Americans what they want.

Sometimes it's legal, like all the Tijuana pharmacies that cater to Americans who cross the border to buy inexpensive medicines. But often it's not. When Californians wanted a drink during Prohibition, they headed south to Tijuana saloons. When American farmers need hands to harvest their tomatoes and broccoli, Tijuana's *coyotes*, human smugglers, find a way to get Mexican workers across, over, under, or around the border's concrete walls and razor wire fences. And for decades, Tijuana's drug traffickers have enthusiastically supplied American consumers with tons of marijuana, cocaine, and heroin.

The Pacific coast city of 1.2 million people is perfectly located to supply illegal drugs to the United States. Cocaine, heroin, and marijuana grown in Colombia and rural Mexico are shipped or trucked to Tijuana, where they are imaginatively packaged in everything from cans of house paint to crates of fresh cheese, to blend unnoticed into the astounding flow of goods and people heading from Tijuana into San Diego. Every year forty-eight million people and eighteen million vehicles cross into the United States from Tijuana, and hidden amid the carloads of people and truckloads of television sets and jeans are billions of dollars' worth of illegal drugs.

The trade produces such vast amounts of money that the men who run it spread millions of dollars in bribes to keep their product moving north. That money has corrupted Mexico to levels that would be comical if they weren't so tragic: Police and soldiers have been caught working as cartel assassins, judges rule as they are told, army generals (including the nation's former drug czar) have been arrested for working with the *narcotraficantes*. The most fearsome drug thugs in Mexico these days, the *Zetas*, are former elite antinarcotics soldiers from the Mexican army. Cops on the street, armed with .38-caliber pistols, don't dare confront their military-issued automatic weapons.

All the money and corruption has led to breathtaking violence. Warring drug cartels have turned the city into a battlefield for years, and literally thousands of bodies have turned up on the streets since Mother Antonia moved to La Mesa. Drug hit men spray their enemies with hundreds of rounds from AK-47s; they massacre entire families for revenge; and in one particularly hideous case a few years ago, they squeezed a DEA informant's head in a vise and popped it like a melon. The drug lord Ramón Arellano Félix was behind much of the violence until he was killed in 2002. At the time of his death, he was on the FBI's Ten Most Wanted list, with his photo right next to Osama bin Laden's.

Thousands of *narcos,* from the two-bit pot smugglers to the big-time kingpins, have ended up on Mother Antonia's doorstep at La Mesa. Many of them are the drug world's expendable pawns. Mother Antonia has known illiterate mothers who were paid a few hundred dollars — a fortune to them — to carry a package of heroin or cocaine on a flight from southern Mexico to Tijuana. When caught, they were sent to La Mesa with the standard ten-year sentence for drug trafficking. Many of the prisoners she has known were young addicts who committed robberies or murder while sky-high on drugs. Others were truck drivers, lookouts, or farmers who allowed their land to be dug up for border drug tunnels or used to stash drugs. In much of Mexico, where even low-paying jobs can be hard to find, many of those people saw nothing criminal about feeding their families by supplying Americans with the drugs they so obviously want.

Once in a while, some of Latin America's biggest drug traffickers have come into Mother Antonia's life. She has sought them out, too, believing that all people are equally deserving of her time and compassion. With their vast wealth, they don't need her toothpaste or pairs of used shoes. But she has found she can help them in different ways, like making them understand the damage that their trade causes, and helping them turn away from it.

"They are just lost in the power and the possessions and the pleasure," she says. "We shouldn't condemn them; we should condemn what they've done."

Her evenhanded approach with the drug

dealers has earned her their respect, as we discovered when we interviewed Benjamín Arellano Félix, Ramón's brother, who U.S. and Mexican law enforcement officials say is the leader and brains behind one of the largest and most ruthless Mexican cartels in history.

Benjamín was arrested in March 2002, when an elite team of Mexican soldiers raided a house and found one of the world's most wanted drug barons cuddled up with his wife in bed. He had never been interviewed by the U.S. press, but not long after his arrest, he agreed to talk to us in the concrete fortress of La Palma prison. We thought about Mother Antonia as we drove there. During most of her years in La Mesa, the Arellano Félix brothers had virtually run Tijuana, and she had known hundreds who had been killed by their gunmen. She had cradled far too many new widows and children in her arms because of them, and they had killed many inmates, police, soldiers, and others she had known.

We were allowed to bring only a notebook and a pen into the prison, and we were thoroughly searched, then led by guards through at least twenty sets of barred doors. Finally, a guard led us down one last empty hallway and pushed open a thin wooden door. Inside, standing totally alone in a cold prison classroom, was a man we recognized instantly from his wanted posters. The United States had a two-million-dollar bounty on his head.

"*Hola.* Benjamín Arellano," he said, holding out a surprisingly small and soft hand to shake. He wore an ill-fitting prison uniform: beige shirt and pants, cheap blue slip-on shoes, and a heavy beige coat. His voice was high and soft, with a slight lisp, and not at all what we had expected from the tough face we'd seen glaring back from so many police photos. He sat at a small table, beneath posters that warned of the dangers of smoking and a chalkboard where the day's English lesson read: "What does Pedro look like? He's fat."

Arellano was about five foot ten, trim, with a bushy black crew cut. The only hint of something unusual were his eyes, which were the color of tar and hooded by thick, black brows. When he spoke, he had the disarming habit of locking eyes with his listener for an uncommonly long time without blinking. He was a man used to intimidating.

He insisted that he was a "simple" housing contractor, wrongly accused, and he ranted about being locked in a six-by-eight-foot cell, where he said video cameras were trained on him all day, even during the weekly conjugal visits he was permitted with his wife. He was upset that there was a light on in his cell all night long, "like I'm a hen they're trying to get to lay an egg."

But then his eyes brightened and his anger popped like a champagne cork.

We had said the right two words: Mother Antonia.

She had given us a message for him: "Tell him I'm praying for him." We told him, and he couldn't get the words out fast enough.

"I've never met her, but I know about her," he said. "She's very famous because she defends human rights. She even lives inside the prison. For her, all people in disgrace are her children."

He leaned forward in his little chair, bubbly for the first time in two and a half hours.

"She's concerned about all people, regardless of their condition, their guilt or innocence. She always finds the humanity in every person. Most people think that if a person is a drug trafficker, they have no feelings. She's a good person, a beautiful person, for prisoners and even those who aren't. She has handed over her life, and she has been doing good for many years."

We asked him if he had any message for her.

"Thank her for praying for me," he said. "I'm a human being like anyone else."

For more than two decades, the name Arellano has meant death to Mother Antonia, a force that shattered so many lives around her. She despises drugs and what they do to people, yet she found even Benjamín Arellano Félix deserving of compassion.

When we gave her his message, she said, "The Arellanos live in a terrible world of darkness." They have expensive clothes and jewelry and cars, she said, and they have the power to control lives, and to end them. But they are haunted by their lives. She has noticed that drug traffickers cannot stand silence. They must always have a television or a radio or music playing. Because in silence, she said, they can hear the truth.

A few weeks after our interview with Arellano, Mother Antonia sent him a Christmas card.

It read, "I'm still praying for you."

In many cases, Mother Antonia's influence with major drug dealers has led to remarkable transformations.

José Contreras Subías was one of Mexico's most successful drug traffickers, moving tons of cocaine and marijuana into the United States throughout the early 1980s with his partner, Rafael Caro Quintero. Intimidation and bribes had allowed them to operate freely since the late 1970s, as they presented many cops and prosecutors with the *narco*'s chilling offer, *plata o plomo,* silver or lead, take the bribe or take a bullet. But things changed in 1984, when Contreras crossed a line with the authorities. The body of a federal police officer was found in Tijuana, stuffed into a car trunk and set on fire. Police were sure Contreras did it, and they went after him.

U.S. officials wanted Contreras, too. He had been indicted in Los Angeles in 1980 on charges of selling a kilogram of cocaine to an undercover narcotics officer, the first installment of a much larger promised shipment. They had arrested Contreras, but he'd skipped town before trial, forfeiting a hundred fifty thousand dollars in bail, little more than pocket change for him.

The DEA's determination to catch Contreras spiked off the charts in March 1985 with the murder of undercover DEA agent Enrique "Kiki" Camarena, whose badly tortured body had been found in a plastic bag in Mexico. DEA informants reported that Caro Quintero had ordered Camarena's kidnapping and then invited many of his drug-dealer buddies to come watch the agent being interrogated and tortured. In an especially ghoulish act, they made tapes of his screams of agony. Because Contreras and Caro Quintero were partners, the DEA assumed Contreras was involved. For the DEA, catching Contreras had now become personal.

It didn't take long. One month later, police in Costa Rica arrested Caro Quintero and Contreras after a shootout at a villa where they were hiding. Mexican authorities flew Caro Quintero to Mexico City, and a judge soon sentenced him to sixty years for Camarena's murder. Contreras was flown to Tijuana and charged, for starters, with murdering the federal police officer whose body had been stuffed in the car trunk. While they held him on those charges, the DEA and Mexican police went to work to see if they could link him to Camarena's death.

Contreras waited in La Ocho. Few in Mexico could believe the news of his capture. Thousands of men passed through

La Ocho over the years, but few of its guests were as infamous as he was, and people came from all over the city just to stand outside and marvel at the thought: They actually have José Contreras in there.

When Mother Antonia heard, she went immediately to La Ocho. Someone of Contreras's stature would be held in isolation, she knew, away from the other inmates, who would be too scared to talk to him anyway. She knew it would be a hard transition, because she had seen it before: a powerful man adjusting to being told when he could eat or go to the bathroom.

The police held back the crowds outside the jail, but they let in Mother Antonia. She found Contreras sitting in a cell and introduced herself by saying, "I have come to bring you comfort from the Lord. You are not alone. You have God's love."

Contreras sized up the small nun standing before him. Strangers rarely talked to him directly, and most people steered clear of him out of fear. He spoke to her softly and respectfully. As they chatted, Mother Antonia tried to reassure him: "God loves you no matter what your charge is."

As Mother Antonia stood to leave,

Contreras told her that her visit meant a lot to him. *"Cuenta conmigo,"* he told her, count on me. I'm at your service. Whatever you need, I'll take care of it. Contreras could easily keep that promise. U.S. officials would later confiscate about twenty million dollars worth of his property and bank accounts in the United States alone, a small fraction of his wealth.

Mother Antonia understood that his offer, *cuenta conmigo,* was no casual remark. He was prepared to give her money for anything she wanted. As she drove home from La Ocho, she started daydreaming about all the things she could do with that kind of help. Maybe it was a gift from God. The money could build a new infirmary filled with medicine. She thought about all the times she had struggled to scrape together thirty dollars for antibiotics for a sick prisoner, or fifty dollars to pay a fine to free someone. She thought about how many lives she could change with Contreras's bankroll.

Then it hit her. She pulled over to the side of the road, furious with herself. She had allowed herself to be seduced for a moment by the thought of all that money. From the moment she started her mission, she had vowed never to accept money

209

earned by selling drugs. Now she fumed at herself for even entertaining the thought, and she knew she needed to set things straight immediately. Turning the car around, she went right back to La Ocho and Contreras. She told him she hadn't come to get anything from him; she had come to give him something: God's blessing. She didn't count on him, she said. She counted on God, and he ought to do the same.

Her anger surprised Contreras, and he told her he hadn't meant any offense and apologized. The moment let them start over and somehow put them on equal footing. Contreras could see she wasn't afraid of him, that she told him exactly what she thought, and that she actually seemed to care about him.

For the next six months, Mother Antonia visited him often, always bringing her message that drug dealing ruined lives. But they also talked about themselves and what led them each to Tijuana. Contreras seemed surprised by her story, but his didn't surprise her at all. She had heard it a thousand times. He had grown up on a poor farm in the mountains that straddle the rural states of Sinaloa and Durango. To escape poverty, he had turned to the easy money to be made moving drugs. His talent for the business aspects of the drug trade had quickly set him apart — he ran like a thoroughbred in a world where the average drug thug was a mule.

Though Mother Antonia turned down his money, Contreras began spending lavishly anyway on improvements at La Ocho. He built a basketball court and fixed up cells and bathrooms. He also shelled out big money to prison officials to arrange for nicer accommodations for himself. The guards obliged and moved a group of mentally ill and drug-addicted inmates to make way for the high-paying customer. When Mother Antonia told him those inmates lost their space because of him, Contreras seemed surprised and said he would pay to not only build a new place for them in the prison, but also a hospital for the mentally ill in Tijuana. He proposed giving the money to the church anonymously, through Mother Antonia, so nobody would accuse him of trying to simply buy himself a better reputation.

Acutely aware of the needs of the mentally ill, Mother Antonia sought guidance from other sisters and priests she trusted, and they all told her that under no circumstances could the church accept money

211

from Contreras. That had always been her rule, too, of course, but she started wondering. Was it really fair to keep a man like Contreras from doing something good with his bad money? She recalled a story a priest had once told her about a pimp who came to him wanting to donate money to the church. When the priest rejected him, the furious pimp said, "Who the hell do you think you are to tell me that I can't do one good thing in my life? You don't have any right to refuse me." The priest told Mother Antonia he had to ask himself if God would refuse someone trying to make amends for a life badly spent. Mother Antonia turned the question over and over in her mind, but the answer still came out the same. For the second time, she refused Contreras's money.

As summer turned to fall, she had many conversations with Contreras and tried to persuade him to get out of the drug business. She had a gut feeling that he was planning to escape; with his money and connections, he could certainly make the arrangements, as many others had before him. One day, as they sat together in his cell, she thought it might be her last chance to get through to him.

"What are you going to say to God," she

said, "when he asks you on your Judgment Day, 'What did you do with all the talents I gave you: intelligence, courage, strength, the song in your heart?' Do you think God would prefer you to say, 'I washed toilets all of my life to help people.' Or, 'I sold drugs that brought into this world an ocean of tears and rivers of blood.' What are you going to say?"

Contreras stood up and paced around the cell, clearly stunned and upset. Mother Antonia had always spoken plainly to him, but never quite so bluntly. He made waving motions toward himself with his hand. "Keep talking, I know I have to hear this. I have to hear it."

She told him to think about the pain he had caused so many people. "Maybe you can't take back what you've already done, but you can change what you are going to do next. Let me remind you, you were not just *in* the mafia, you *were* the mafia. You were not just a *capo,* you were the *capo de capos.*"

"It hurts me to hear you say that," he said, still pacing like a tiger. No one had ever challenged him to take a hard look at himself, and now when he did, he didn't like what he saw.

She didn't let up. She told him he should

use his fame to warn people about the dangers of drugs and the violence of a trafficker's life. Young men looked up to him as a hero. He could change their lives if he wanted to, and he could change his own. She told him everyone deserved a second chance, and he should take his.

Contreras stopped pacing and looked at her. He told her she was right. He knew it. "I'll never sell drugs again," he told her. "I'll never have anything to do with drugs again."

Then the big drug lord got down on his knees and asked her, "Bless me, Mother." She made the sign of the cross over his head, and he told her, "How could I ever forget what you told me?"

Whether or not he would actually keep that pledge, Mother Antonia felt sure he had reached an important turning point, like an alcoholic finally admitting he has a problem.

A week later, on October 25, 1985, Contreras escaped and crossed the border into San Diego. Six guards and the prison warden were later charged with helping him. He left a note for the police with a taunt that became famous on both sides of the border: *Me voy a Disneyland.* I'm going to Disneyland.

A few days later, a tall Mexican man who introduced himself as Joe Guillén bought a million-dollar ranch in rural Atoka County, Oklahoma, about a hundred twenty miles northeast of Dallas. He told his new neighbors that he had inherited some money. Contreras, now known as Joe, continued running his drug empire from Oklahoma, despite his promise to Mother Antonia. DEA agents also continued hunting for him, and three years after his escape from La Ocho, police arrested him in Salt Lake City. He was convicted in federal courts in California and Oklahoma on drug-trafficking and money-laundering charges and sentenced to twenty years in prison.

He was never charged in the death of Camarena, the DEA agent. Despite exhaustive forensic examinations of the house where Camarena was tortured, the DEA never found any evidence — not a hair, a fiber, a fingerprint — that Contreras had been anywhere near Camarena.

While serving his time in Lompoc federal prison in California, Contreras had plenty of time to think. He would later say he thought over and over about what Mother Antonia had told him. He began reading the Bible and spent time with Evangelical Christian missionaries who visited the prison, and he eventually began teaching Bible study classes himself.

In August 1998, after a decade in prison, authorities released him for good behavior and immediately deported him to Mexico, where was sent back to La Mesa to face the still-pending charge of murdering the federal police officer. When Mother Antonia heard the news of his return, she went to see him. As she arrived at his cell, he stood up and embraced her, excited. He told her he never forgot the lessons she tried to teach him, and that they finally sank in during his years in Lompoc. He had been raised believing in an eye for an eye, and he said it took him many hard years to understand that he could be forgiven for his crimes and that he could forgive others. He said he was a changed man.

"I know the law of God," he told her. "I never knew it before, but now I know."

He had not quit drug trafficking the first time he promised to, but Mother Antonia believed he would now.

"Maybe he hadn't figured out how to stop the drug business yet," she says. "Maybe he thought he would be killed if he stopped. I think it's like the alcoholic who says, 'I know how alcohol has ruined my life and I'll never take another drink.' And all they can think of is getting back to the bar."

Contreras was released from La Mesa in March 1999, after less than a year, and moved back to his home in Tijuana with his wife. Mother Antonia kept in regular touch, meeting often with him for breakfast, and he became a helpful adviser to her about what she called her "heavy cases." His background made him the ideal consultant for how to best help inmates in trouble with drug dealers. He also started devoting himself to charity works, funding numerous construction projects, building churches and centers for drug addicts, and setting up training centers to teach them carpentry, plumbing, and other skills. He tried several times to enlist businesspeople in Tijuana to help him, but they didn't want to be associated with him. Mother Antonia understood their objections but thought people like Contreras deserved a second chance.

But those are hard to come by in the violent culture of the Mexican drug trade, and even though Contreras had abandoned the drug world, it caught up with him on August 30, 1999.

As he was driving home with his mother and daughters, he spotted a Chevy Suburban with smoked windows — the drug assassin's vehicle of choice — following him. Driving into his garage, he told his family to get inside the house quickly and he stayed behind in the car, leaving the garage door open. He apparently didn't want the killers to fire randomly through the closed door and put his family at even greater risk. Police found his body in the driver's seat. He had made no attempt to get away or fight, and they found no drugs or weapons in his car or his home.

Mother Antonia was crushed by the news of his death. She had hoped he would outlive her and keep spreading the message that there is always a better life for anyone who seeks it.

Although Contreras could never quite free himself from the violence of drugs, another former inmate Mother Antonia has known for nearly thirty years has managed to earn a most unusual status: retired drug lord. Robert Hernández was once the chief heroin supplier to the United States, but now, blind and in his mid-seventies, he lives the clean, quiet life that Mother

Antonia pushed him toward for years.

Robert and his wife, Helen, were pioneering heroin smugglers with connections from Lima to Marseilles. They were the Bonnie and Clyde of the 1970s heroin trade, right down to Helen's Faye Dunaway blonde, take-your-breath-away looks and a pistol on her perfect hip. But now Helen is long gone and hardly anyone knows that Robert is still alive; he is a living page of history, as if legendary mafia figure Meyer Lansky were discovered today painting pretty seascapes in Havana.

"I been straight for eighteen years," Robert says, speaking in his old-style gangster English, filled with "dis" and "dat" like a character from an Edward G. Robinson movie. "Nobody else coulda done that but Sister Tony." Robert and Helen were the only people who ever called her that.

In their heyday, Robert and Helen owned mansions with tennis courts and swimming pools and private shooting ranges. Robert once traded a half-million dollars' worth of heroin for a 140-carat diamond-and-emerald necklace for Helen. They both came from rough beginnings. Robert grew up in the East Los Angeles barrio of Boyle Heights, and his abusive father was sent away to an asylum when

Robert was only a year old. He spent his childhood on the barrio's tough streets and eventually ended up in a juvenile jail for slashing a man with a broken bottle. Helen's story was similar. When she was still a baby, her mother went to prison for forging checks. Helen landed in juvenile detention when she was fifteen and was arrested again when she was twenty-three, along with her mother, for more check forgery. She might have gone straight when she was released two years later and took an office job, but she was fired when the boss found out about her record. "I went to jail for two years for robbing twenty-five dollars," Helen fumed. "I paid society for that. Why do I have to be judged for the rest of my life?" Seeing no better option, she turned to the drug business.

Robert and Helen met in Los Angeles in 1957, were married almost immediately, and moved to Mexico in 1959 to start in the drug trade. For the next decade, they built an operation that cops would come to describe as the General Motors of the heroin-trafficking industry. Then, in 1968, Robert was arrested in Tijuana on a weapons charge and ended up in La Mesa, a hot-shot gangster with L.A. sophistication and Tijuana brass *cojones*. When an article appeared in a local newspaper one day naming him and eleven other men as the "Dirty Dozen," the biggest *narcos* in town, a local drug trafficker named Patricio Becerra was jealous and decided he was going to get rid of the Dirty Dozen.

A few days later, a hit man hired by Becerra came up behind Robert in La Mesa, put a pistol to his head, and fired twice. One slug came out Robert's eye, and another came out his jaw. Then the thug put three more shots in Robert's back, and the guards and the warden left him lying there on the ground, like a dying animal.

Helen arranged for a neurosurgeon who had been part of the team that worked on Senator Robert F. Kennedy, who had been fatally shot just months before in Los Angeles, to come to Tijuana to assist in the surgery to save Robert. He was in a coma for twenty-three days, and when he awoke, he was blind, but even that couldn't keep him from his work. When he was released from La Mesa not long after the shooting, he and Helen, now joined by his brother Johnny, kept building their business. During those years, Robert carried a live grenade for protection, taking it out in meetings and tossing it up and down in his hand like a baseball. The sight of a blind man juggling a live grenade tended to unnerve people. Helen used to say, "Most wives say to their husbands, 'Don't forget your lunch box.' And I would say to Robert, 'Don't forget your hand grenade.' "

By the 1970s, their operation was so notorious that President Richard Nixon ordered federal authorities to shut them down, and Mexican President Luis Echeverría did the same. Robert hired famed L.A. defense attorney Barry Tarlow as his lawyer in the United States.

In 1970, Mexico City's police chief, Arturo "El Negro" Durazo, the country's most feared — and spectacularly corrupt — law enforcer, came to Tijuana to personally arrest Robert, Helen, and Johnny. After they were convicted on numerous charges, Robert and Helen set up housekeeping in La Mesa's *El Pueblito* and continued making deals over the phone. One of the biggest drug rings in the hemisphere was now headquartered in a one-room *carraca* in La Mesa.

Business boomed until October 1974, when an elite team of Mexican antinarcotics police raided Robert and Helen's *carraca,* where they grabbed thirty-six thousand dollars in cash and a quarter-million dollars' worth of diamonds and jewelry. The surprise raid also netted Robert and Helen's notebook filled with the names of their contacts and details of their smuggling routes, and their operation was smashed for good.

By the time Mother Antonia arrived in La Mesa in 1977, Robert and Helen's business was in ruins, and Helen was suffering from what would later be diagnosed as uterine cancer. Almost immediately, Mother Antonia and Helen spotted each other and started spending time together. Mother Antonia listened to stories of Helen's childhood and wondered how her life might have turned out differently if that office job had worked out, if people had been more forgiving. Helen was fascinated by Mother Antonia, carefully observing how she turned her few real tools — her personality and persistence — into huge amounts of donated goods. "Sister Tony, you're in the wrong racket," Helen told her. "You shoulda been a con woman."

Her courage especially impressed Robert. In June 1978, four heavily armed inmates shot and killed La Mesa's warden, assistant warden, and two guards; four inmates were also killed in the cross fire. The incident had started a few days earlier,

Robert says, when one of the prison's worst troublemakers, high on crystal methamphetamine, was shooting at a cockroach with a smuggled-in pistol. Backed by guards, the assistant warden came to his cell and took the pistol from the inmate in front of his family, who were staying with him. "You're gonna insult me in front of my family?" the furious inmate yelled at the official. He stayed high on crystal for the next three days, plotting his revenge, which ended in the massacre. The shooter and his accomplices were handcuffed, and behind La Mesa's walls, where guards could do as they pleased, they were mercilessly beaten. The guards stood them up in buckets of water and gave them electric shocks to the testicles. Mother Antonia, who had been outside the prison when the killings happened, banged on the door and tried to get them to stop. She almost always could, but this time it was like trying to stop feeding sharks. Robert heard her pleading with the guards to stop the beatings. The brutality went on for three nights, and Mother Antonia never gave up. Robert knew tough gangsters, but that was the bravest damn thing he had ever witnessed.

In 1979, Robert was released from La

Mesa, three years early for good behavior; Helen still had time to serve. Mother Antonia kept in touch with him, persistently urging him to start a new life. On New Year's Eve, he wanted to go visit Helen, who was alone in La Mesa and not feeling well. He asked Mother Antonia for a ride, and she remembers telling him that night, "I think you've already paid for your crimes. You've already been to hell. Your Annie Oakley is all punched out."

When she was growing up, the local ballpark would give out a card and punch it once for each admission. The holes were supposed to look like bullet holes from Annie Oakley's gun. When the card was all punched out, you got in free. "When you get to St. Peter's Gate," she told Robert, "you tell them your Annie Oakley is all punched out."

His response seemed totally out of character for tough-guy Robert, almost childlike. "Sister Tony, you think that's true, that there's time for me to be God's good son again?"

She told him there was always that chance, for anyone, but he had to ask forgiveness for his sins. He agreed, and she called Father Rasura in San Diego, who came across to Tijuana and sat with

Robert for a long time and emerged with a smile. He said he made a good confession.

Not long after, a woman came to the prison and told Mother Antonia she feared for her husband's life. He had given some information to the Mexican police, and now she was afraid the Hernández brothers were going to kill him. Mother Antonia went to Robert. He was furious. He hated snitches more than anything, and he told her, "Sister Tony, there's only one way to handle that kind of thing." She knew exactly what he meant, and she was horrified. "Robert, God just forgave you for all the sins of your whole life," she said to him. "Now you've got to forgive just one person."

"Sister Tony," he said, "I come from the old school, where they kill you if you talk. They put a gun in my mouth, Sister Tony, right in my mouth, and I don't talk."

Mother Antonia understood his philosophy, but that didn't make it right. She said revenge was wrong and only perpetuated the violence. Robert apparently listened to her, because nothing happened to the snitch.

After Helen was released from La Mesa in 1980, suffering terribly from her cancer, they took the risk of crossing the border into San Diego to seek treatment for her. Before they reached the hospital they were picked up by U.S. authorities on a long list of drug-trafficking charges. Sentenced to ten years each, they were sent to the same prison in California. But not long after, Helen was moved to a different prison for medical care, and Robert would never be with her again. Helen passed away in 1984 in prison after calling Mother Antonia to ask that she watch over Robert. "This is going to be hard on him," she said. "And just pray that God forgives me."

Robert was released two years later, and when his parole was finished in the United States, he quietly slipped back into Tijuana, a forgotten man. Now he lives alone in a small apartment, with no decorations except a portrait of Helen that he can't see on top of a television he can only hear. His stake in a little car dealership earns him spending money.

By the time Robert returned to Tijuana, a flashier, bloodier generation of traffickers had taken over the industry, dominated by the Arellano Félix gang, famous for their AK-47 assault rifles. Robert's mansion near the golf course in Tijuana is long gone, and the beach property he owned near Puerto Vallarta ended up in the hands of a well-connected politician, as things often happen in Mexico. He thinks he still might have some money stashed away somewhere; he remembers stuffing a lot of money into bank accounts, maybe in Ciudad Juárez. He's not really sure, and he doubts he'd be able to find it anyway. Surely somebody's already stolen it.

"It's just as well," Mother Antonia says to him. "That was bad money, and you're better now."

They were sitting together in Casa Campos, sharing breakfast and a cup of tea, two unlikely friends in their mid-seventies. They both once had high-flying lives in Los Angeles, but they no longer did, for dramatically different reasons. Now they sat in a small Tijuana dining room comparing aches and pains and reminiscing about all their shared years.

"How much did it cost you to be the Godfather?" she asks him.

"Too much," he says softly, behind his black sunglasses. "Too much."

Rigoberto Campos Salcido paid an even higher price.

Rigo came from a little village in Sinaloa state in northwest Mexico, famous for what grows in its year-round sunshine: delicious tomatoes, and a fantastic abundance of bright green marijuana and the brilliant red poppies used to produce heroin. A Sinaloa farmer can work dawn 'til dusk picking tomatoes for two dollars or grow drug crops that bring in as much as two thousand dollars on a single harvest day. Thousands have done the math. As the drug trade took off in the 1960s and 1970s, many Sinaloans made millions and became Mexico's new rich. In the eyes of thousands of boys like Rigo, they were heroes. Many were lionized in folk songs, called *narco-corridos* — later several would be written about Rigo. In places like that, Mother Antonia has seen over and over, the lure of drugs is too tempting for many to resist, even for people who have the ability to succeed in legitimate businesses.

Rigo was a magnet of a man when Mother Antonia met him in La Mesa in 1978. Everybody wanted to be near him. He stood six foot one, with wintergreen eyes and rare charisma. Other inmates marveled at Rigo's vocabulary and wardrobe as much as they feared his reputation for toughness.

Born into a large family in a village with no electricity or running water, Rigo left home at fifteen, in 1967, paying smugglers a hundred dollars to bundle him across the U.S. border in the trunk of a car. He was going to live with relatives in Los Angeles, but his ride ended just over the border, where the smugglers dumped him on the side of the road, literally barefoot and penniless. He eventually made his way to L.A. and enrolled in public school and learned English. To earn cash, he hauled furniture for a moving company, but before long he figured out he could earn a lot more hauling something else.

He was good at smuggling, and his business grew rapidly until 1978, when he ended up in La Mesa for a few months on a marijuana-trafficking charge. Mother Antonia met him almost immediately, and they spent a lot of time together. He enjoyed talking to her about his Catholic faith, and she liked his big personality.

Before he was released, Mother Antonia urged him to take himself in a different direction. "Make yourself a good life. You have so much going for you," she said, telling him he had the brains and wit to be a great businessman. He stayed in touch with her by phone over the years and told her he had been "doing good things." But then, in 1986, he showed up again at La Mesa, once again arrested on drug charges.

Now thirty-four, he had grown prosperous and wore the most expensive jeans and always a freshly pressed shirt. Poor inmates, who follow the big traffickers the way some kids follow their favorite sports stars, trailed him around the prison yard, and he passed out cash to them.

Rigo told Mother Antonia that he was also working as an agent for Interpol, the international police agency. She believed him because his ability to speak both English and Spanish and his knowledge of the drug business might have made him attractive to them. She had also heard from another drug dealer that Rigo was playing both sides of the fence and needed to watch himself.

Not long after Mother Antonia had gotten to know Rigo, her daughter Elizabeth, who had inherited her mother's blonde beauty, came to La Mesa for a visit. It was her first trip to the prison. She had recently been divorced from rock musician Ron Blair. At twenty-five, she was raising a two-year-old son and working as manager of a boutique on Rodeo Drive in Beverly Hills, the weight of single parenthood pressing down on her. She needed some time with her mother. So she left her son with relatives and drove to Tijuana, staying a week in the prison and sharing her mother's tiny cot. She was upset when she saw where her mother lived and how she showered in icy water. But when they walked together through the prison yard and the men swarmed around, calling out *Madre! Madre!,* Elizabeth could feel how their affection warmed her mother more than a thousand hot showers.

On that first day, she and her mother ran into Rigo, and Elizabeth thought he was unusually charming. She was even more taken by him the next day, when dozens of red roses arrived for her at Mother Antonia's *carraca,* and the two started a romance. Elizabeth was lonely and Rigo was alone. They talked about their lives and loves, and Elizabeth found herself thinking about Rigo after she returned to L.A. He immediately made his intentions clear. The day after Elizabeth left, he appeared at Mother Antonia's cell all dressed up and made a startling announcement: "I am in love, Mother. I want to marry Elizabeth."

Mother Antonia had seen and heard a lot in prison, but that stunned her. She liked Rigo, but she hadn't brought Elizabeth to the prison to meet men. Before long, though, Elizabeth returned to La Mesa to see him and then started making frequent visits. When Rigo was released a few months later and returned to a ranch he owned in Sinaloa, he and Elizabeth stayed in constant touch. He told her he had left the dope business and wanted only to be a farmer now, talking about how much he loved the land and working in the fresh air. That was the life, he said, that he had always wanted.

Elizabeth went to visit him at the ranch, realizing that she had fallen in love with him. She thought he was a wonderful person who had made some terrible choices. But in her days there, she also began to realize that even if he had walked away from his criminal life, his enemies and rivals would not leave him alone. When he left the ranch, he always had one car full of bodyguards in front of him and one behind. Scores are settled in the drug underworld, no matter how old they are. So as hard as it was, Elizabeth called off the relationship.

Rigo stayed in contact with Mother Antonia, not letting his heartbreak over Elizabeth change their relationship. He met her for breakfast or lunch when he traveled to Tijuana. During those talks, he assured her he would never go back to the drug business. But he also told her he and his family were still in danger.

One day not long after that, Rigo's uncle Manuel opened his front door in Sinaloa, and assassins shot him to death. Weeks later his brother Tommy, a father of eight children, was killed in a spray of automatic gun fire right in front of Rigo's mother. Rigo knew the killings were a message to him, and he told Mother Antonia he worried that the infamous "settling of accounts" wouldn't stop until his whole family had been killed. He seemed to grow more spiritual as he felt the danger closing in. His conversations with Mother Antonia increasingly focused on God and faith, and he always asked her to bless him.

He had also started to give away a good deal of his money, supporting two hundred families who lived nearby or worked on the ranch. He told Mother Antonia he wanted to build a house for poor women and children visiting La Mesa prisoners. He had seen how they had to sleep in the bus station or on the street as they waited to visit their husbands and fathers, and he knew Mother Antonia struggled to find them places to stay. So he paid one hundred thousand dollars to buy a small house two blocks from La Mesa and he gave it to Mother Antonia. He showed her receipts and other paperwork to prove to her that the money had come from his growing ranch business — not from drugs, but from alfalfa.

Rigo thrived on the hard work of the farm, which reminded him of his youth. He switched more and more acres from corn, the traditional crop, to the more profitable alfalfa. Mother Antonia visited occasionally and once made tortillas with Rigo's mother. During those visits, he and Mother Antonia talked a lot about forgiveness, about not allowing yourself to be overrun with rage and hate, and Mother Antonia pleaded with him to forgive the men who had killed his uncle and brother. She told him that hatred and vengeance are a cancer, and forgiveness is the only cure.

Rigo's life seemed to be taking a turn for the better, but then it fell apart on a January day in 1990. He was on the ranch, using an industrial auger to dig holes for fence posts. As the machine noisily chewed into the rocky earth, a string on his windbreaker got caught in the corkscrew bit. In a second, the powerful, spinning machine pulled him down to the ground and ripped off both his arms between the shoulder and the elbow. He collapsed in a bloody heap. Panicked ranch hands grabbed a blanket and wrapped him up, trying to stop the gushing blood, and rushed him to Almater Hospital in Mexicali. When doctors pulled the blood-soaked blanket off Rigo they looked for the arms, thinking they might be able to reattach them, but in their panic, the workers had neglected to bring them. They raced back to the ranch to retrieve the arms, but it was too late.

Word spread instantly that the famous drug lord, as they called him in newspapers, had lost his arms. Swarms of federal police staked out the hospital looking for associates of Rigo who might come to pay their respects, or for enemies who might come to kill him. The police and DEA said, and still believe, that rival traffickers cut off his arms. The story became an instant legend in the press: Gangsters were now mutilating each other in new and more horrible ways.

When she got the word about Rigo, Mother Antonia rushed to Mexicali. Rigo made it out of surgery alive, and when he awoke, she was there. He looked down to where his arms used to be and, horrified, he turned to her and said, "Mama, I don't want to live."

"You have three wonderful reasons to live," she said. "You have your mind to think with, a heart to love with, and your soul to be saved."

"I'll never be able to hold my daughter in my arms again," he cried out, and burst into tears.

She told him it could always be worse, that it could have happened to his daughter and not him.

"What if she couldn't put her arms around you?"

Pulling a wooden bench up next to his hospital bed, she laid a blanket on it and slept there for several nights. The heavily armed federal police outside Rigo's room were puzzled about why she cared so much about a man they saw as nothing more than a drug thug. They advised her to leave, because she would be in the line of fire if someone came to try to kill Rigo. But she stayed, sleeping in her habit and not leaving his side.

In the weeks that followed, Rigo tried to adjust to a life in which he could not comb his hair, drive a car, feed himself, or clean himself in the bathroom. He was just thirty-eight. His new prosthetic arms were awkward, and he avoided public places. He felt humiliated by his new helplessness.

But even that wasn't enough for his enemies. A year later, assassins came after his family again, this time for Rigo's older sister, Adelita. They shot her to death in Sinaloa as she carried a bag of groceries from her car. Rigo couldn't attend her funeral because he knew he would endanger his family by being there. Mother Antonia offered to go in his place, but Rigo wouldn't have it. "They are wiping out my family," he told her. "And you are considered family." He said she needed to stay away from him now, that she could easily be standing too close to him when the killers came.

But she could not stay away in the moments when he needed her most. If fear dictated her actions, she never would have moved into La Mesa. Rigo was in such despair over his sister's murder that Mother Antonia feared he would seek vengeance, and so she sat with him in a quiet room at the ranch and told him to forgive, to let it go. "Nothing is so noble as to forgive something so serious," she told him. "If you kill these hit men, you are in danger of losing your soul." She told him to look out the window at the clouds that were there one second, then swept away by the winds. That is life: fragile and temporary. Use the short time you have been given to make a difference and to do good, she told him. Don't waste it on violence and vengeance.

Five days after his sister's death, on February 26, 1991, Rigo called all the remaining members of his family and workers together on the ranch. "*Se acabó. Se acabó la bronca,*" he told them, the fight is over. "No more guns. No more vengeance. We are not going against those who killed my family."

The next day Rigo took a rare trip off the ranch to drive into Tijuana to have a look at some horses that were for sale. He and five bodyguards drove in two large sedans, and the killers, who had apparently been watching Rigo's movements, were waiting for them. Eleven of them sat in two vans positioned near a downtown exit ramp where Rigo's cars would have to slow down. They pumped one hundred twenty-three bullets from AK-47 machine guns and .45-caliber pistols into Rigo's two cars. Rigo was reclined, maybe sleeping, in the front seat of one of the cars, and they hit him with forty bullets. In the end, Rigo and four other men lay dead, covered with blood and a carpet of shattered glass. Ricocheting bullets also killed the teenaged daughter of a Tijuana politician and wounded several other bystanders. The Tuesday afternoon execution shocked even murder-weary Tijuana, and the killers have never been caught.

When Mother Antonia heard the news, she went immediately to the morgue, where the five bodies were laid out on cold tables. Rigo's body looked tranquil. She stroked his hair and prayed for him. A policeman saw her and said, "I'm sorry Mother, but I don't care that he got killed. These are *narcos* killed by *narcos*. There's an innocent girl who was killed, and she's the one I care about." Mother Antonia knew that most of Tijuana felt exactly that way, and she mourned the loss of the girl, too. But she also knew there was much more to Rigo than what appeared in the newspapers.

Crowds of people from all over Baja California turned out to mourn the politician's daughter. Local television stations covered her enormous funeral and reported that her death stood as a tragic and shameful reminder of how good people are killed on the fringes of Tijuana's raging drug wars. Only family and Mother Antonia went to a small private service for Rigo.

The house Rigo bought near the prison

has become Mother Antonia's headquarters and office. Thousands of women and children have slept in the clean, bright dormitory-style rooms upstairs. Some are visiting family members; some are just-released prisoners. Lines of people come and ring the bell at the front gate, looking for a job, something to eat or drink, or just a place to sit for a while. The house has one rule: No one is ever turned away.

The house is named Casa Campos de San Miguel, after Rigo Campos and St. Michael the Archangel, a drug dealer and an angel.

TEN

NOT FORGIVING IS HARDER

Every year, on Ash Wednesday, Mother Antonia makes her way around La Mesa with pens and paper.

She asks inmates, guards, the warden — everyone she can find — to write the name of someone they can't forgive: a parent who treated them badly, someone who stole from them, someone who did them wrong, anyone who did something that hurt them that they can't forgive or forget. She asks them to write just the name, or to write out the whole story if they want. She tells inmates who never learned how to write to mark the paper with an X. Then she lights a fire in a big cast-iron kettle in the prison chapel, and the prisoners come one by one to drop their letters into the flames.

On the altar in the prison chapel, she and a priest rub the ashes from the burned letters on prisoners' foreheads. Then she takes her small cup of ashes with her all day and hits every forehead she can find, in visits to police stations and hospitals and street corners all over Tijuana. It's a tradition that she started in 1979, which she calls the Day of Forgiveness.

This is Mother Antonia's inventive protest against the eye-for-an-eye logic that dominates prison culture, where one murder is avenged by another and then another, until no one can remember what started the cycle. She believes forgiveness is far more effective than any punishment at controlling all the hate and homicide. The violence stops only when someone decides to forgive. She believes that's as true inside La Mesa as outside, where grudges held and slights remembered poison family relationships and friendships unnecessarily for years.

"Forgiving is hard," she says, "but not forgiving is harder."

The desire for revenge is a burden that crushes, because it becomes an obsession. "Unforgiveness will age me, it will make me sick, and it will make me ugly," she says. "Nothing can bring me so low that I'm going to not forgive somebody and destroy myself. Because that's what unforgiveness does. It's a boomerang that comes back."

Her words can sometimes be difficult to accept, but as Mother Antonia has witnessed many times, they help people overcome terrible pain. Mother Antonia has sat beside dying men and asked them to forgive their attacker so they don't die with the burden of hatred. She has told women whose husbands or sons have just been murdered that their pain will pass more quickly if they forgive the killer.

Griselda Robles was one of Mother Antonia's closest friends, almost like a daughter to her. They had met in 1977 when Griselda was working as an administrator at Tijuana's General Hospital, and she vividly remembers her first glimpse of Mother Antonia: "I was in the information booth at the hospital, and suddenly I saw this nun. She was radiant. Just seeing her, I felt happiness and energy."

Ten minutes later, Griselda ran into her again. Mother Antonia appeared to be looking for something, and from the sound of her Spanish, she was a foreigner who was a little lost. Griselda asked her in English if she needed help.

"Oh, you speak English?" said Mother Antonia, who had only recently arrived in Tijuana. "You're the angel I was asking God to send me. I thought I could speak

Spanish, but now I realize I can't, because no one understands me."

Griselda helped Mother Antonia on her errand that day; she was trying to find a metal plate for an inmate who had broken his leg and needed reconstructive orthopedic surgery. From then on, the two worked closely at the hospital, and eventually Griselda took a one-year leave of absence from her job to work full-time with Mother Antonia. She saw her teach forgiveness many times, but it really hit home on May 13, 1984.

Griselda's twenty-four-year-old nephew, Sergio, was leaving a liquor store when he ran into a guy from the neighborhood known as the Squirrel, who tried to steal the bottle of tequila Sergio had just bought. They fought, and the Squirrel stabbed him in the heart with a screwdriver.

The family was devastated. Sergio was a good kid who had managed to steer clear of the Tijuana drug trade, but it caught up with him anyway. The police concluded that his killer, who was about Sergio's age, had been high on drugs when he committed the murder.

Mother Antonia had seen so many families torn apart after such a tragedy, the drive for revenge and a burning hate consuming them and creating more misery. She went to see Sergio's mother, Griselda's sister Alicia, and along with offering her sympathy she also urged Alicia to let her anger go. "Sergio had a great family, a great mother, a great father, and great friends," she told her. "But the man who killed him never had that. He never had a nice birthday party, someone to love him, someone to hold him. He didn't have any of the same opportunities in life that Sergio had." She said the Squirrel was not a man to be hated, but one to be forgiven, that while hatred and revenge might seem as natural as exhaling after inhaling, they are destructive.

Alicia found comfort in what Mother Antonia was saying. "She was my protection and my help," Alicia says now, twenty years after the killing. "She told me, 'I know you are suffering terribly, but you must forgive Sergio's killer.' I knew what she was saying was right, and from the very first moment, she gave me the strength to say, 'I forgive him.'" She was especially moved by what Mother Antonia said about the killer's mother. "I thought about her, and how she was suffering like I was," Alicia says. "I think we were suffering the same pain, from different causes."

Mother Antonia proposed a public gesture of forgiveness at Sergio's funeral, in which she would represent the Squirrel's mother, who could not be found. The two mothers stood before Sergio's casket, holding hands to show, Mother Antonia says, that, "We were both mothers, and we had both suffered tragedy. We both lost a son, one to death, and one to shame and horror."

Not everyone in the family liked the idea. Alicia says her husband was so angry that she feared he might beat her for saying that she forgave Sergio's killer, and her brother José was furious, too. After the funeral, José stopped Mother Antonia in the church.

"Why are you honoring a murderer?" he said to her.

Mother Antonia said she understood how he felt, and that she knew he and Sergio had been extremely close.

"I can't forgive him," he told her. "Sergio was like my son, and that punk killed him for no reason. I won't forgive him."

There in the church, Mother Antonia got down on her knees in front of José.

"José, I'm begging you. There's nothing we can do to change the act. We can only

247

change what is in your heart. If you can't pray for him, don't pray against him. Please let go of your burden of hate. The boy will be paying for what he did for the rest of his life, but you will be, too, if you don't forgive him."

José helped Mother Antonia to her feet, overcome by the sight of her on her knees. "It's okay, *Madre*. It's okay," he said.

After the funeral, a man approached Alicia's husband and said that for two hundred dollars, he could arrange to have the Squirrel killed in prison, the way such things are so often settled. Alarmed, Alicia called Mother Antonia, who went to see her husband and talked him out of considering it. She told him that having the Squirrel killed would be as evil as killing Sergio. Mother Antonia kept talking to Alicia's husband and José, and both of them, in time, came to believe that she was right. "They both got over their feelings of hate, because of Mother Antonia," says Alicia, now sixty-seven and living in Chula Vista, California.

Forgiveness is not just something Mother Antonia urges for other people; it is something she has had to practice many times in her own life when her close friends have been victims.

A slight, silver-haired man in his mid-sixties, Jesús Blancornelas may be the toughest journalist in Mexico. He founded his weekly newspaper, *Zeta*, in 1980, just three years after Mother Antonia arrived in Tijuana. *Zeta* made waves instantly in a country where officials had long been accustomed to gentle treatment from the press. Reporters and editors regularly took bribes from politicians to write glowing stories about them. But Blancornelas took money from no one, and he started writing boldly about the corruption and drug trafficking that infested the city. He and Mother Antonia, both crusaders challenging conventions in a city and country where change comes slowly, became good friends. He calls her "an oasis of purity in the midst of all the tragedy, corruption, and disgrace."

Blancornelas has paid a heavy price for his work. In 1988, gunmen killed one of his two partners, Héctor Félix Miranda, who wrote columns that examined the business of the Arellano Félix drug cartel and their friends in government. Bodyguards for Jorge Hank Rhon, a multimillionaire who was elected mayor of Tijuana in 2004, were convicted in the killing. (Jorge Hank Rhon was never implicated or charged in the murder and denies any involvement.) In June 2004, one month before that election, another *Zeta* editor was killed. Francisco Ortiz Franco was shot to death in a car with his two young sons sitting in the backseat. Ortiz had recently begun work on a new investigation into the Félix Miranda killing; his murder remains unsolved.

Blancornelas's relentless pursuit of drug traffickers and their involvement with government officials earned him countless threats over the years and almost killed him after he ran a front-page story about a man named David Barrón. Blancornelas put his photo on the cover in November 1997 and identified him as an assassin for the Arellano Félix cartel. A few days later, gunmen ambushed Blancornelas's Ford Explorer and sprayed several dozen rounds into the car. His bodyguard, Luis Valero, was killed, and Blancornelas was struck five times.

Blancornelas, wounded and bleeding, saw one of the gunmen, wearing gloves and a bulletproof vest, approaching him with a pistol, presumably to inflict the *"tiro de gracia,"* the cartel's signature single shot to the head, a well-known drug world symbol of a revenge killing. But another of the killers continued firing at Blancornelas's car, and one of his bullets ricocheted and struck the gunman approaching Blancornelas in the eye, killing him instantly.

It turned out to be David Barrón.

When Mother Antonia heard about the shooting she went to the hospital, where Blancornelas was under heavy guard and in critical condition. The bullets had done severe damage to his liver and lungs, and one had lodged close to his spine.

Mother Antonia sat with Blancornelas's wife, held her hands, and urged her to forgive the shooters. "If you could forgive the men who shot your husband, great good would come to this world," she said. "There is so much hate. If you could forgive them, it's going to help your husband to live because it will be a blessing for him. The act itself is unforgivable. But it would be wonderful if you could forgive the men who did it."

Blancornelas's family was moved by Mother Antonia's plea; it made sense to them that vengeance would make nothing better. When Blancornelas was feeling stronger, Mother Antonia made the same argument to him, and he says it was the only thing anyone said to him in those painful days that rang true. "Everybody else who came to see us said, 'These are such bad people.' Then all of a sudden someone is telling us, 'Forgive them, forget it. Don't live with rancor,' " he says. "She was right. There is no reason to keep living with hate. And in reality, after she was close to me and my family, that's how it's ended up. I don't feel hate, and it doesn't anger me."

Mother Antonia also went to say a prayer over Barrón's body, despite what he had done. "I knew nobody else would be allowed in to see him, and maybe no one else would want to," she says. So Mother Antonia went to the city morgue, where doctors had just finished performing his autopsy. There were nineteen skulls tattooed all across his torso, and police told her that each represented a person he had killed.

She touched Barrón's hair. "He had one eye with the long lashes and the other eye that was blown out. All I could think was, 'What happened to him in life?' "

What she knew of Barrón's dark résumé — assassin for the Arellano Félixes — told her much about who he was. She had seen it many times in La Mesa. "I'm sure he didn't belong where he was born. So he found a place to belong in the gangs. And when they started using him as a hit man, that's when he became famous. He finally found a place where he could say, 'I belong. I don't belong in school. I don't belong with friends. I don't belong in church. I don't belong in my family. But I belong here. These are my guys. They are my kind of men, and I will die to be with them. I'll kill to be with them.'" A bad childhood was no excuse for the violence and pain he had caused. But she went to the morgue to ask God to have mercy on him.

She returned to Blancornelas and told him what she had done and, as she says, "The beautiful thing about Jesús Blancornelas is that he didn't feel a bit bad that I went down to bless the body." In fact, he admired her for it. "It is wonderful that Mother Antonia goes to those people and rescues them," he says. "She comes to be with me, blesses me, embraces me. And then a little later she goes and embraces a drug trafficker. This is her labor and her way of thinking. All the people, the *narcos* and us, we all love her. She is a miracle that repeats itself every day."

Blancornelas recovered from his wounds and still publishes *Zeta*. The newspaper's office is always guarded by at least a dozen police and soldiers, who accompany him everywhere.

Mother Antonia often meets the killers of her friends in La Mesa. She confronts them with the enormity of their actions and tells them they cannot be forgiven unless they ask for forgiveness. That was the message she brought to the men who killed Alfredo de la Torre Márquez, Tijuana's municipal police chief.

She had known him for years. He had been head of the guards at La Mesa and then warden, before becoming police chief. De la Torre would have made a good politician, she thought, because he was warm and funny and had a commanding presence. He was a chain-smoker who hid his cigarettes from her, because she was always scolding him about the dangers. She even bought him a nicotine patch. When the young son of a guard came down with leukemia, they both offered to donate blood to him; they were both type B-negative — another bond.

When de la Torre was named police chief in December 1998, Mother Antonia was troubled. Four years earlier, police chief José Federico Benítez López had been ambushed and killed by drug gangs. She asked him not to accept the job, but he said he had no choice. "I'm a cop," he told her, "I have to do it."

On Saturday, February 26, 2000, de la Torre, who was forty-nine, went with Mother Antonia to a downtown event for *Brazos Abiertos,* the fund she started for widows and orphans of police. He seemed uneasy, unusually serious, not his normal gregarious self. She noticed that he was being careful not to stand too close to his wife, and she asked him what was wrong.

"Mother, if I live through this, I'm going to join with you," he said.

She didn't understand what he meant. She touched her veil and asked him if he meant join with her, as in join in her mission work. He said yes, that he wanted to help her in her work, particularly to help police officers. Because he seemed so nervous, she called him later in the day, worried that something dangerous might be going on. But he downplayed it, saying, "It's nothing. I'm a cop. It's always like this."

The next morning, Mother Antonia was coming back to her cell from morning prayers and a guard stopped her and told her, "Alfredo de la Torre has been shot."

The news tore through her, and she shook with emotion. The guard took her to see her friend Apolinar Aguilar Nieto, the head of the guards. She demanded of him: "Tell me the truth! Is he dead? Tell me!"

But no one wanted to give her such sad news.

A guard drove her to the hospital. When they arrived, there were police everywhere. She saw a lawyer she knew coming out of the hospital. "It's over," he said. "He's dead."

An autopsy showed that de la Torre had been struck by fifty-seven bullets. He had been on his way to the office that Sunday morning after attending Mass by himself. He normally traveled with several bodyguards, but he had given them Sunday off. The killers attacked him from three large vehicles, one of which pulled in front of his Chevrolet Suburban to slow him down, while two others pulled up beside him and started shooting.

Mother Antonio believes de la Torre was worried that he was being hunted and purposely went to Mass alone so that nobody alongside him would be killed. Maybe the cartels had offered him a bribe that he wouldn't accept. Maybe there was something else going on that no one knew about. Either way, she is sure that he knew he was in danger, so he kept his family at a safe distance.

When she arrived at the funeral home the next day, his body had already been dressed in full uniform and prepared for burial. Mother Antonia approached the casket and looked at her friend. She put a copy of her Prayer for Police in his hands. Then she took the cross from around her neck and laid it on his body.

De la Torre's funeral Mass drew a large crowd, including high-ranking officials from President Ernesto Zedillo's administration and law enforcement officials from Mexico and the United States. Tijuana's mayor pleaded for "an end to this climate of horror." The FBI ran ads in Spanish-language newspapers in San Diego and Los Angeles offering a reward for information about de la Torre's killing. Within days, seven men, including a former Tijuana police officer and another city employee, were arrested and charged with the murder. The hit was reportedly carried out on orders from "El Mayo" Zambada, whose organization was in a bloody turf war with the Arellano Félix gang. After the men were arrested, they were brought to La Mesa.

Mother Antonia went upstairs to where they were being held. They were accused of fifteen murders, including de la Torre's, and the police had beaten them badly during interrogations.

"You can't just say 'I'm sorry' and make this go away," she told them, saying they needed to look into the faces of the children who no longer had a father and feel their pain. One of the suspects, a young man who appeared to be about nineteen, couldn't stop crying as she spoke. She sat with him and told him he must make it clear to God that he understood what he had done, that he accepted the enormity of it, and that he was truly repentant.

"Maybe belonging to the mafia seemed important to you," she told him. "Maybe having those big heavy weapons and the women and the money made you feel ten feet tall. But you are somebody because you are God's child. And none of the rest of it means anything. Look up into the sky and see a billion planets, and you'll see what power is. It doesn't come from a wallet or a weapon."

She held the young man in her arms and he sobbed into her shoulder. Moving among the other men, she held each one of them, and then she asked them all to pray with her. It was cold in the room, so she went to find them some coffee and blankets.

The police guarding them had seen the

whole thing. And when she went outside into the hallway they just stared at her. She knew what they were thinking: *You were like a second mother to Alfredo. How can you be so kind to the men who killed him?*

She looked back at them.

"Are there any of you here who have clean hands?"

No, they said. None of them could claim to be without sin.

"Okay then, these men are cold. Could you get them a cup of coffee?"

They got the coffee, and Mother Antonia went back to her *carraca* and scooped up all the blankets she could find, including the one off her own bunk. Early the next morning she stopped in to check on the men, who greeted her with broad, relieved smiles.

"Mother, we slept," they told her. "We all slept for the first time since they arrested us."

Later in the day, Mother Antonia turned on the television news and saw the seven men, chained together, being led up the steps to a plane that was going to take them to La Palma prison. She knew they were going to be locked away for many years.

As she watched on television, she saw

the youngest, the nineteen-year-old who had wept on her shoulder, turn toward the cameras just before he entered the plane. He was crying. She couldn't hear him, but his simple words, which he said over and over, were easy to read on his lips:

Estoy arrepentido.

I repent.

Mother Antonia believes in forgiveness because she is sure there is goodness in everyone, no matter how hardened they've become or how hard it is to see. She has helped many La Mesa inmates find their better sides, including a tough young surfer from California named Robert Cass.

Robert grew up on the southern California coast, filled with anger and attitude. His mother died when he was young, and his father was abusive. By the time he was nineteen, it seemed like a good idea to steal a sailboat in San Diego. He was caught and given probation. He was sure he could do better a second time, so he stole another boat. He was convicted again.

Before sentencing, in May 1981, he strapped a surfboard to the top of a rusted-out Volkswagen Bug and steered south until he hit the little Mexican coastal village of

San Blas, the perfect little patch of no-where for a guy looking to hide from the police and smoke dope in the sunshine. He told everyone his name was Richard Schumacher, and he passed the months living in a beachfront *palapa* and surfing, often with Pancho, a friend's pet spider monkey, clinging to the front of his board. On his first day in town he met a pretty young local girl, Margarita, and they eventually started dating and opened a small restaurant together.

Before long, he joined the drug trade that was everywhere around him. One day in 1986 a Mexican couple asked him to help them move about a hundred grams of heroin across the border, and he drove with them to Tijuana, where they were all caught by the local police. Robert passed a terrifying night in a cold, wet cell, listening to the screams of men being tortured by the police, including the man in the next cell, who had battery acid poured on his genitals.

First thing the next morning, a small nun came walking down the row of cells in the police station, speaking what Robert thought was some of the funkiest gringo-Spanish he had ever heard, and he thought, *What the hell is this? She must be lost. How did she get in here?* He didn't talk to her that morning; he didn't want spiritual help, he wanted somebody to get him out of there. Eventually he was sentenced to eight years and four months in La Mesa. He was twenty-six, and his life had gone to hell.

In the prison he became a "real hard case" who smoked pot, revved himself up with cocaine, then popped downers to get to sleep. He got into countless fights and was stabbed several times, and his tough-guy attitude made him a regular target for beatings by the guards. He fully intended to go back to smuggling when he got out of prison, but this time with a whole new set of powerful connections he had made inside. Even while still locked up, he set up meetings between Mexican drug smugglers and U.S. buyers on the telephone, taking a small cut for each transaction.

Margarita, his girlfriend from San Blas, didn't give up on him right away, and came twice for conjugal visits. She became pregnant on the second visit, and she gave birth to a son, Robert Abraham. She came once to see Robert when the boy was eleven months old, but she never returned. Robert careered through his late twenties trying to make sense of a life that seemed to make none. And everywhere he looked, he ran into Mother Antonia.

One morning in 1989 the state judicial police conducted one of their periodic raids on the prison, in which they confiscated the money, jewelry, and drugs so many prisoners kept in their cells. This time the fed up inmates decided to rebel and started throwing empty Coke bottles at the police. As the rain of bottles pelted down, guards opened fire, two prisoners fell dead and many others were wounded.

Then Mother Antonia walked through the gate. With her arms held up high over her head, she walked into the middle of the flying bottles and bullets. Inmates and guards screamed at her to stay away, but she just kept walking, saying, *"Mis hijos, mis hjios.* Stop this. You must stop this now." And the scores of police and guards and hundreds of rioting inmates put down their weapons. The yard went quiet. The fighting ended. Robert couldn't believe that she had survived, let alone stopped the riot.

Not long after, Robert found himself going to Mother Antonia's cell for the first time to talk. All the violence of life in La Mesa had worn him down, and he felt shattered. They talked for more than an hour. He told her he felt worthless, horrible, the worst of the worst, that his life felt like one crisis leading to another, and that there must be something inherently wrong with him. He didn't think there was any good in him.

Mother Antonia told him to think back, way back, to when he was six years old. She asked him to remember that boy, to remember the joy and innocence of youth, to try to see that little boy and to pick him up in his arms. She told him to open his heart to him and take another look. Was that boy terrible and worthless? He had lost one parent and been abused by another. He wasn't bad, she said; he was just a child in pain. He had goodness in him then, and still did.

Robert realized she was telling him that goodness is an eternal quality, not something you have and then lose. Bad behavior and poor choices might have masked it, but they couldn't take it away. *Am I really this person I've become?* he thought. *Or am I something better?*

His change of heart would still take some time, though. At Mother Antonia's urging, he started reading the Bible, curious about where her strength came from. But despite his affection for her and his newfound curiosity about faith, his dreams of narco-dollars were still stronger than what the psalms were selling. "I read the whole Bible, Old Testament and New," he says. "And I just thought it was a load of crap."

Then he went through an experience that brought Mother Antonia's teaching home to him.

In July 1990, Robert took part, with sixty other inmates, in a hunger strike at La Mesa to protest torture by police — the strike that had brought Rubén, the young man whose intestines were stomped so mercilessly by the police, to her attention. Robert ate nothing for fifty-one days and developed pneumonia and a serious lung infection that left him almost unable to breathe. Doctors in the prison infirmary treated him with antibiotics, which were a rarity in those days. He believes prison officials went to great effort to save him because they didn't want the bad publicity from a U.S. citizen dying there. But they gave him such massive doses that he had a reaction that caused his joints to freeze up. He couldn't bend them for several days. It was the worst pain he had ever felt.

Mother Antonia came to see him every day, bringing him soup, but he was still honoring the hunger strike and refused to eat. She held his hand and told him about Bobby Sands, the Irish Republican Army rebel who had died on his hunger strike a few years earlier, stressing the futility of it all. She said no one has the right to take his own life, and she told him he had lots of reasons to live. But he told her he was too tired to go on, that he'd been in the prison for too long to care any more about life.

In time, though, her words started to get through to him, and he began reexamining things, trying to figure out where he had gone so badly wrong. He came to a simple realization. Mother Antonia had urged him to understand that he was there because of bad choices he'd made, not because he was a bad person. He hadn't been able to see the difference before, but now he felt an overwhelming calm come over him, because he finally knew, "It's not everybody else's fault. It's my fault that I got myself here, and the beautiful thing about that is that I can choose not to do that anymore."

After he had been in the infirmary about a week, Mother Antonia came in and they sat together on the bed. She had given him a small King James Bible that he kept with him in the infirmary. She picked it up and said, "Let's see what God has to say." She opened it at random and read the first lines she saw, which said that a wise son listens to his mother. She laughed. "See," she said, "you're supposed to listen to me." Then she opened to a different page and read a verse about how love can make even the most humble meal taste good. They laughed again. "See, I love you and you're supposed to eat." She won him over.

Just give in, he thought, *I can't fight this anymore.* Mother Antonia once again brought him some soup, and he started eating. That moment was the beginning of a long and difficult process of choosing a new life for himself.

Three weeks later Robert left the infirmary and started working with Mother Antonia, first in the infirmary, cleaning it up, giving it a coat of paint, making sure patients always had a pitcher of clean drinking water. A raffle he organized raised five hundred dollars to install a new ventilation system to help slow the tuberculosis and other illnesses that spread there. He started going to the *Grito* every morning with Mother Antonia, or even when she wasn't there, distributing clothes and hot food to the scared new prisoners.

On Thanksgiving Day 1990, more than

four years after his arrest, the warden called Robert into his office, where Mother Antonia and an official from the Mexican parole board waited. "I've got some news for you," the warden said. "You are the first foreigner to get parole from a Mexican prison. I have never seen someone so completely changed."

He was released the next day, but he still had other debts to pay. With Mother Antonia's encouragement, Robert gave himself up to U.S. authorities, who still wanted him on the charges he jumped bail on years before. Now officially Robert Cass, he spent the next six months awaiting trial in a federal jail in San Diego, where he read the Bible again, and this time, he says, it finally made sense.

Mother Antonia came to San Diego to testify on Robert's behalf at his sentencing hearing, and instead of getting the maximum of twenty-five years, Robert got twenty-four months. He was sent first to a federal prison in Texas, and while there the years of trauma in La Mesa caught up with him and he suffered a nervous collapse. When he got himself back on track, he started volunteering in a prison hospice, caring for dying prisoners. In May 1992, after serving eighteen months, he was released for good, one month short of his thirty-third birthday.

Mother Antonia found Robert a bed in the St. Vincent de Paul shelter in San Diego. Even when he moved into a small apartment, he continued volunteering at the shelter and eventually began managing a much larger, seven-hundred-bed shelter. Once in a while, his duties included taking large loads of donated food and clothes to La Mesa, but he gave that up because being back in the prison was "weird, totally weird."

In 1996, Robert enrolled at San Diego State University and emerged five years later with a bachelor's degree and a degree in nursing. In 2000, he went to state court in San Diego to apply for a "certificate of rehabilitation," a document that is one step short of a pardon. Mother Antonia testified on his behalf before the judge — the same judge who had been on the bench in 1981, when Robert skipped out on his second sailboat-stealing conviction.

"Sister talked to him for me. And the judge was so happy for me. He was reading my story, and he said, 'You're working at the Health Department? And you're co-ordinating this study, and you're going to nursing school? This is great! I wish you all the best, let's stamp this thing.'" Robert took a job as an intensive care nurse at a San Diego hospital, where he still works.

Robert and his wife, Annie, a consultant for the California Health Department, now live in a bright suburban house in San Diego, high on a hill with a view of the Pacific Ocean and a Volvo and an SUV parked in the driveway. Sitting on his back patio with a lovely trellis and a big grill, Robert thumbs through a box of memories from his days in Mexico. It is filled with photos of him during his long hair and lamb-chop mustache days in San Blas and with letters to and from Mother Antonia. There is also his King James Bible, with its worn blue-leather cover, that Mother Antonia gave him fifteen years ago. Nearly every page is underlined and highlighted.

Annie says she sees Mother Antonia's influence on her husband every day. "She allows you to move beyond where you've been and say, 'Okay, where am I today, and what positive choices can I make from this point forward?' Once you've had contact with her, you carry her with you. Whenever we have to decide something big in our life, we always ask, what would Sister want us to do? She's like a little Lojack that's with you all the time."

Robert Abraham, Robert's son who until recently had lived with his mother in Mexico, now lives with Robert and Annie in San Diego. He is president of his high school's surf club and competes on the team, which his father coaches. Annie and Robert now have two more children, including their firstborn, a daughter named Bridget Antonia.

"My story would be a lot different without Sister," Robert says. "I'm afraid to even think about what it would have been like without her, and I did all that time on my own, never seeing her, never hearing her say, 'I love you, *hijo*. You're a good person, no matter what.' Somebody needs to be in there telling people that they're okay, that they're good people, and that the things they've done don't totally define who they are."

ELEVEN

ANGEL ON CALL

Passengers arriving at the Tijuana airport are greeted by life-size photographs of the city's leading citizens, including famous artists, writers, and Mother Antonia. Her inclusion in the "Faces of Tijuana" exhibit, which opened in 2002, is another sign of the growing recognition of her work. She has won dozens of civic awards in Mexico and the United States, including the American Academy of Achievement's Golden Plate Award, which has also been awarded to several U.S. presidents, civil rights pioneer Rosa Parks, director Steven Spielberg, and Hamid Karzai, the president of Afghanistan. As Mother Antonia's reputation has grown, government authorities have turned to her for help in their biggest criminal cases.

While she was visiting prisoners in the federal police headquarters in Tijuana one day in 1994, a commander asked her to please help two distraught women in a visitors' room. As she began talking to them, she discovered they were the mother and sister of the man just arrested for killing Luis Donaldo Colosio, a presidential candidate assassinated the day before.

Colosio had been a shoo-in to be the next president of Mexico. On March 23, 1994, just a few months before the election, three thousand people turned out to hear him speak at a rally in Lomas Taurinas, a poor neighborhood near the Tijuana airport. Forty-four and charismatic, Colosio stood on a makeshift podium in the bed of a pickup truck and promised to deliver a "government closer to the people." When he finished and stepped down from the truck, people pressed in close to him, wanting to shake his hand and touch him. Dance music blared loudly, and Colosio smiled and reached out eagerly into the pulsing crowd. Then a young man put a .38-caliber revolver to the candidate's head and blew his brains out.

Colosio fell to the ground, bleeding, eyes staring blankly, and the man fired a second shot into his stomach. Colosio's bodyguards and others in the crowd pounced on the shooter and held him down. Panicked police struggled to get him out of the crowd before he was lynched amid frenzied cries of "Kill him! Kill him!"

Colosio was rushed to a hospital and pronounced dead three hours later. Suddenly no one knew who would be the next president of Mexico, as no other candidate was even close to him in the polls. Rumors of conspiracy whipped through the country, as many believed the assassination was not the work of a lone gunman, but the result of a dark power play within Colosio's Institutional Revolutionary Party, known by its Spanish initials PRI.

President Salinas urged the nation to remain calm as he met the Mexican military plane carrying Colosio's body to Mexico City. He then named Colosio's campaign manager, Ernesto Zedillo, as the PRI's new candidate, and when Zedillo was elected later that year he was known as the "accidental president."

Days after the assassination, Mario Aburto Martínez, a twenty-three-year-old factory worker from Tijuana, sat bruised and bloodied in La Palma prison, more than fifteen hundred miles from his home, where he had been flown under heavy guard after the shooting.

Immediately, stories started appearing in the press that raised doubts about whether police had the right man, even though Aburto was the man wrestled to the ground by the crowd. Newspapers ran police mug shots of him alongside photos taken of the shooter at the scene. Was it really him? What about the hair? Can we really be sure it's not a double? Ever-wilder conspiracy theories spread throughout Mexico, and they included everything but a grassy knoll.

Mario Aburto Martínez's family was in shock as hordes of reporters camped outside their small home in Tijuana. Mario's mother, María Luisa Martínez, had been questioned by the police but could offer no explanation for her son. She kept saying he had been doing well at his new job, operating machinery at a factory that made cassette tapes.

Mother Antonia could see how frightened María Luisa was to be swept up in an assassination that changed Mexican history. She invited her large family to come to Casa Campos to recover from their shock and stay out of the limelight. A dozen family members moved into the rooms upstairs, and they helped out around the house, washing dishes and clothes, cooking, and emptying the garbage. María Luisa kept busy with her hands, tatting —

a form of embroidery. She made a table-cloth for the dining room table and a cloth for the altar in the house's small chapel.

"I don't know what happened," she told Mother Antonia again and again. "It must have been an accident."

Mother Antonia also tried to be sure Mario's brother stayed alive. He was serving time in La Mesa, imprisoned for lack of paying a small fine, and she feared other inmates might harm him because his brother had killed Colosio. As she won his release, he told her Mario had always pushed him to work hard so he could have a better life. Study, study, study, Mario had told him. How else are you going to crawl out of poverty and become something?

As days passed, pressure mounted for María Luisa to speak publicly. Mother Antonia was having a harder and harder time holding off the journalists. Mario's father, Rubén Aburto, who lived in the United States, returned to Tijuana and gave several interviews, saying that Mario was innocent and suggesting that there were "others involved." But he offered no names or evidence to support those allegations. The press was determined to hear from María Luisa.

Mother Antonia persuaded her to hold a

news conference, where she could say that she was as confused as anyone else about why her son pulled the trigger. She told María Luisa that the pressure on her would ease after she spoke, and she could return home.

In a room filled with lights and cameras and microphones, María Luisa held Mother Antonia's hand as she told a listening nation: "I don't know. I don't know why he killed him." They asked again and again, she answered the same way, and then it was over.

The family returned home, but the speculation about the killing continued, and some even questioned whether Mario was still alive. No one had seen him publicly since the shooting, and even some officials in Tijuana who came to talk to María Luisa told her they doubted her son was alive. The federal police had probably tortured him to death for his crime, they said. María Luisa was terrified, but Mother Antonia assured her that if there was one person the Mexican authorities wanted alive, it was Mario Aburto. The whole world was watching, and the last thing President Salinas wanted was for the shooter to turn up "accidentally" dead in police custody.

But to make her feel better, Mother Antonia arranged for her to visit her son and bought two tickets to Mexico City. As the plane climbed, María Luisa pointed out the windows at the clouds and asked, "Is that snow?" She had never been on a plane, nor ever learned to read or write.

She told Mother Antonia about the pain of working barefoot in strawberry fields when she was a young girl, when many times the only food her family had was stale, hard tortillas and black coffee.

As a young woman, she embroidered tablecloths. A woman from Mexico City would come to her village in Michoacán state and give her the thread and cloth. She knew that what she sewed was sold for much more money than the pittance she was paid, but she figured a few pesos were better than no pesos. She told Mother Antonia she was proud that her family had worked hard and had never stolen anything despite their poverty.

When they arrived in Mexico City, Mother Antonia went to the office of the federal attorney general, Jorge Carpizo, where officials who knew her made arrangements for María Luisa to visit her son in the prison the next day. That night they ate in an inexpensive Chinese restaurant near the hotel, and María Luisa remarked that what the two of them spent for dinner could buy her whole family food for a week.

María Luisa asked Mother Antonia to come with her to the prison. She was afraid there might be some kind of trick, that the police might be waiting to arrest her. The two women passed through one set of iron doors after another into the bowels of the prison. Mario was waiting in a small, sparsely furnished conference room. He wore a prison-issue beige jacket and pants, and his dark hair had been cut short. He had gained some weight since his arrest, but he was still of average size and build, an unremarkable-looking young man in the most remarkable of circumstances.

"Mother," he said, warmly, standing and embracing María Luisa.

But rather than return his embrace right away, she asked him, "Do you still have your cross?"

"¡Mamá!" he said in shock, "Don't you know it's me?" realizing that his own mother was asking him to prove his identity. He turned around, took off his jacket, and lifted up his shirt, showing a small, cross-shaped scar on his back — the result of a childhood fall. María Luisa had been so shaken by all the talk that Mario had been killed, or that police were holding a double, she wasn't even sure of her own son.

Mario pulled his shirt back down and said to his mother, "I never want you to come back here again. And tell my brothers and tell my dad, I don't want any of the family coming here to see me. I'm afraid for every one of you. Get out of here and go to the United States."

Mother Antonia tried to tell Mario that no one would hold his crimes against his mother. But Mario didn't believe it. He said Aburto was not a common name, and his relatives would always be tainted because of what he had done. He told her that the family should forget him and stay away from him. Then Mario turned to Mother Antonia, fixed her with a serious look, and told her his story, about how a series of unplanned events led him to Colosio's side.

He said he had bought an old handgun because he lived in a tough neighborhood where there were many robberies. But he had second thoughts and worried that maybe his little sister might find the gun and hurt herself. He had tried to sell it to a friend, but the friend didn't want it.

He looked at his mother, and said, "You remember that, right?"

She said she did.

So Mario decided to take the gun to work to see if he could sell it to someone there. He tucked it into his jacket and went to the factory. But when he got there, he worried that he might lose his job if someone saw him flashing a gun around, so he kept it to himself. When he got off work that afternoon, a friend told him that Colosio was holding a big rally in town. He said, "Hey Mario, you like politics. Why don't you go down and see this guy, the next president of Mexico."

So he went. Mario told Mother Antonia that when he arrived the crowds were already huge, and he got caught up in the jostling and ended up being pushed and pushed until he was almost right next to Colosio. The gun was still in his jacket pocket.

He told Mother Antonia that as he watched, he saw a poor young man trying to get Colosio's attention to hand him something, perhaps a letter or some kind of written petition, as Mexicans frequently do with visiting officials. Mario said Colosio ignored the young man and then he saw Colosio, or maybe one of his bodyguards, physically brush him back. Mother Antonia thought that was odd. Presidential candidates on a campaign visit to a slum don't intentionally offend a poor supporter. But Mario was insistent about what he had seen: Mexico's wealthy political establishment treating the poor like dirt.

"Did that bother you?" she asked Mario.

"Mucho," he said darkly. *"Mucho."*

He told Mother Antonia he was angry at Colosio, at what he represented, at all the ways the poor in Mexico suffer at the hands of an indifferent elite.

"I wanted to scare him, so I shot," he said. "I thought, 'How would you like somebody to push you back?' The gun was in my hand, Mother, and I shot. But I thought I shot at his feet."

Mother Antonia was amazed. The country was convulsed with complicated theories of political conspiracy. The public had still not heard Mario's story, and here he was telling her that the assassination that had shaken the country was the result of a moment of unpremeditated rage.

"I did it, and they won't let me talk," he said. "They won't allow me to tell anybody. The thing I don't want is for somebody else to be blamed. They're saying it was a conspiracy. There was no conspiracy, and I don't want other people to go to jail for something I did."

Mother Antonia felt for him. He was so young and so angry and hurt, but she still admonished him.

"You took the life of a man, Mario," she said, "He's dead. And he was the hope of Mexico. Everybody was looking for a new kind of leader, with youth and vitality and honesty and caring. Their hope was really in this man."

"I'm sorry, but that's the way it was," he told her. "I didn't go thinking I was going to kill anybody."

Mother Antonia believed him. She had spent decades with convicts who had tried to deny their crimes, and Mario seemed to be speaking directly from his heart when he said a lifetime of feeling oppressed had erupted in an instant of rage. She could feel the hate that had been roiling inside him for years.

Mario clearly wanted to tell the world that he had acted alone and that no one else should be blamed. So Mother Antonia went back to Carpizo's office and reported what Mario had said, and she also told Bishop Berlie, who had given Colosio the last rites in Tijuana's General Hospital, and many reporters as well.

She also instinctively felt she should keep one detail secret. She never mentioned what Mario told her about why he had pulled the trigger, how Colosio or a bodyguard had supposedly pushed away a poor person who wanted to give him something. At the time, she felt it served no good purpose and could stir up emotions in an already volatile atmosphere. But more than a decade later, she now wants the whole story to come out, to add to the record and understanding of a defining event in modern Mexican history.

Mario Aburto Martínez was convicted later that year of murdering Colosio and was sentenced to forty-five years in prison. Mexico has no death penalty or life sentences.

In October 2000, after one of the most thorough investigations ever undertaken in Mexico, the federal government concluded that Mario acted alone. It reached that judgment after officials conducted nearly two thousand interviews and compiled more than sixty-eight thousand pages of evidence. Announcing their findings at a news conference, Attorney General Jorge Madrazo Cuéllar and other top officials described Mario as a paranoid man who harbored grudges against politicians because of the failures in his own life.

Mother Antonia believes what motivated Mario was sad and simple: hard tortillas and black coffee.

Three years after Colosio was shot, Mother Antonia found herself in the middle of another case that made international headlines.

After Mass at the San Miguel church in Tijuana one weekday in March 1997, a stranger came up to her in tears. The woman said everyone in the city knew Mother Antonia helped anyone in trouble, and her husband was in a lot of trouble. The woman introduced herself as Rosalinda Navarro and explained that her husband, Army General Alfredo Navarro Lara, a fourth-generation Mexican general whose great-grandfather led Mexican troops against the French at the famous Cinco de Mayo battle on May 5, 1862, in Puebla, had been arrested.

Mother Antonia, of course, knew of the case. It had been sensational news in Mexico and the United States. Navarro was accused of offering a bribe on behalf of the Arellano Félix cartel to the top army general in Baja California. Mexicans are accustomed to official corruption, so it wasn't the bribe that shocked them. It was the amount.

A million dollars a month.

"I'll see what I can do," Mother Antonia told her.

When General José Luis Chávez became the army's top official in Baja California in February 1997, he was the ranking law enforcement officer in the busiest drug corridor in the country. Almost immediately, he sensed that something was not quite right about General Navarro, an old family friend. Navarro had called him several times and seemed extremely nervous, so when he called one day to ask for a meeting to give Chávez some "important information," Chávez was deeply suspicious. So he put a microcassette recorder in his pocket. He put a clip into his pistol, switched off the safety, put two more clips into his pants pocket, and walked toward the hotel where Navarro wanted to meet. Just before he got there, he turned on the recorder.

Navarro was waiting for him in the parking lot, nervously puffing on a cigarette. He led Chávez to a suite in the hotel. He said someone from the cartel had asked him to offer Chávez a bribe to look the other way as drug shipments went through Tijuana, and that he had refused. Then Navarro got a call saying men were parked outside his house, and their guns were trained on his pregnant daughter, Adriana. The caller told him to make the offer to Chávez or they would start shooting. "All we have to do is pull the trigger," he said.

"They forced me to come to see you," Navarro told Chávez, talking very fast. "They are threatening my daughter and my family."

"How much are we talking about?" Chávez asked.

"A million dollars a month," Navarro told him.

Chávez was stunned, both at the size of the offer and that it was being made by a general. He believed Navarro's story that the drug dealers were threatening to kill his family, and he was sympathetic. But not that sympathetic. As he walked out of the hotel, he checked his tape recorder to make sure he got it all. Within hours, the tape was on its way to the attorney general's office in Mexico City, and Navarro was arrested and sent to La Palma.

Rosalinda asked Mother Antonia to come with her to speak with her devastated husband.

"I have disgraced our family name and the flag of Mexico," Navarro told her when they met at the prison. He said his only solace was that his daughter and new grandson were alive. "I know that they wouldn't be living if I hadn't made that offer."

Mother Antonia, aware of the painful tumble that Navarro's well-respected family had taken, spent a couple of hours with Navarro that day, and returned for two more visits. She pleaded on his behalf before the judge in charge of his case. She asked for a light sentence, saying Navarro had made a mistake under terrible pressure. With international attention focused on the case and the Army's integrity on the line, the judge sentenced him to twenty years.

Rosalinda now lives with Adriana and her young son, Anthony, in a small apartment in the United States just south of San Diego. Adriana supports the family with her job as a ride operator at the San Diego Zoo.

"Mother Antonia is a force," Rosalinda says. "She has a light, and those of us who are suffering follow it. Every time I am in a state of crisis, I just talk with Mother and she calms me. I feel like I have known her for a thousand years."

While Navarro was awaiting sentencing, General Chávez called Mother Antonia to help with the aftermath of the most horrific crime he had ever seen: the massacre of seventeen members of a single family. The only survivors were two traumatized children, and although they had been assigned an army psychologist, Chávez said what they really needed was Mother Antonia, because "she is a vision of God in a place of perversity and evil."

The killings occurred at a ranch near Ensenada, a coastal town about sixty miles south of Tijuana, on September 17, 1998, and the army had taken the two children — one of them badly wounded — into protective custody at a military hospital there. Chávez was one of the first officials to arrive at the ranch, and he was shaken by what he saw — two hundred and fifty shell casings scattered in a pool of blood more than an inch deep. The fetus of a pregnant woman was exposed in the line of bodies ripped open by the shooting.

The killers had broken into the El Rodeo ranch, a gated property with three houses, satellite dishes, and show horses grazing in the field, and pulled eighteen members of Fermín Castro Ramírez's family out of their beds. The gunmen had forced them to lie facedown on a concrete patio and executed them with Kalashnikov rifles, shotguns, and pistols. The dead included seven children still dressed in pajamas or their underwear.

In weeks after the killings, police pieced together the story. The ranch was owned by Castro, a small-time drug smuggler who had gotten on the wrong side of the Arellano Félixes by refusing to pay a "tax" for operating in territory they controlled. Thirteen armed men, who had been drinking and snorting cocaine, arrived at the ranch just after four in the morning.

According to Chávez, the massacre started with a moment of rage when one of the Arellanos' lieutenants, Lino Portillo Salazar, found Castro in his bedroom and pulled him into the hallway to demand payment. Castro punched Portillo, who responded by shooting Castro once in the head. He left him bleeding on the floor. In his rage, he then ordered his men to pull everyone else in the three houses out onto the patio.

Viviana Castro, one of the survivors, woke to the sound of a struggle outside her bedroom.

"Don't move or I'll kill you!" a man yelled.

Viviana, fifteen years old and seven months' pregnant by her young boyfriend, listened from her bed, terrified.

"Is there anyone else in the house?" he yelled.

She heard her mother's voice, calm and level, saying, "No, there's nobody else here."

Tiptoeing barefoot to the door of her tiny bedroom, she quietly pushed it shut. When she heard heavy footsteps coming closer, she hurried to hide behind a dresser. A man pushed the door open, filling the room with bright light from the hallway. He looked around and then crouched down and looked under her bed.

Viviana prayed over and over, "Please, God, don't let him see me." The room was so bright, and there was not enough space to hide. But somehow the man with the gun didn't see her and walked out of the room. Too terrified to move, she stayed behind the dresser, and minutes later she heard long sprays of gunfire.

After the shooting ended, Viviana stayed hidden for another half hour until she heard someone coming through her front door downstairs. Instinctively, she thought it was her mother and ran out of her room and down the steps, calling *"Ma, Ma."*

What she saw horrified her. It was her cousin Mario, a chubby eleven-year-old, dazed and covered with blood. He told her

291

what happened. "Everyone is dead," he said. He had been shot twice, in the arm and leg, and his chest was cut open by flying shards of concrete kicked up by all the bullets. He had played dead among the bleeding corpses of his family until the killers left. Viviana couldn't believe it and ran back upstairs, looking for anyone else who might be alive.

She was frantic. Mario was losing consciousness, and she tried to keep him awake, afraid that if he passed out he would die. Holding him up, Viviana led him to the house of a neighbor, who drove them to the hospital in nearby Ensenada. Chávez moved them to a hospital on a secure military base and posted soldiers outside their door. As eyewitnesses, they were in grave danger. There had been bigger body counts in the past, but the Ensenada massacre had violated all the unwritten rules of the drug world. Never before had so many women and children been executed, a new benchmark for brutality.

Mother Antonia was driven to Ensenada from La Mesa in a military jeep. In a brightly lighted first-floor hospital room, she found two children looking blank and hollow. Mario was wrapped in bandages, and the two had barely said a word. "I want you to know that my heart is broken, too, for you," she said. She talked about how wonderful heaven must be, and how their parents and relatives were surely there. After a while, she asked if she could hug them, they said that would be okay, and she rocked them in her arms.

Mother Antonia spent most of the next month with Mario and Viviana, talking to them, trying to comfort them. She was concerned that they were not showing any emotion. She wanted them to cry and scream and get their pain out. She brought them a VCR and funny videos to make them laugh and a radio so they could listen to music. She brought them teddy bears, too, which Mario didn't want at first.

When a soldier guarding the door walked in, Mother Antonia held up the bear for him to see.

"Sergeant, how would you like to sleep with this in your arms?" she asked him.

The sergeant understood right away what she was up to.

"Oh, let me hold that," he said, taking the bear into his arms with a big, theatrical hug. "Oh, does this feel good! Oh it feels so good! Mario, lend it to me because when I take my nap I want to hold onto it."

Then another soldier came in and started hugging the bear. "Oh, it feels good. It really feels good!"

When Mother Antonia came back to the room later, Mario was lying on the bed, sound asleep, with his arms wrapped around the teddy bear.

At the same time Mother Antonia was making daily visits to the children, she was taking regular trips out to the crime scene, where a group of suspects was being held. The army had rounded up some men for questioning, and they were using the ranch as the headquarters for their investigation. Mother Antonia asked Chávez for permission to visit the men. Like a doctor who is obligated to set a broken leg whether the patient injured it by being a hero or committing a crime, she believes her role is to comfort all those who need it, regardless of why.

Still, she felt this was a test of the limits of her compassion. Arriving at the ranch, she was horrified by the dried pool of purple-black blood covering the patio. She entered one of the houses and found a half dozen men under guard. They were not handcuffed, and she could tell by looking at them that they had not been tortured, which pleasantly surprised her.

"I'm Mother Antonia, and I'm here to serve you," she said to them.

She told them, in the understated words she so often uses for those suspected of murder, "If you did this, you did not spill a cup of coffee on the rug. You can't just say, *'discúlpame, perdóname.'*" She told them that if they had killed these people, or even made a telephone call that helped the killers, they must grieve for the pain they had caused. The men listened with their hats in their hands, many of them looking down at the floor in shame. She had brought them rosary beads and prayer books and asked each one if he needed anything. Some talked about their children; some knelt and asked for her blessing.

Mother Antonia returned several times to the ranch. Sometimes the same men were there; sometimes new ones were added. As the police continued their investigation, Viviana and Mario still had not been able to give them any information about what they witnessed. Mother Antonia knew the children were afraid, and she told them, "The whole world wants to protect you and knows you are two special children." A friend of hers who was visiting China had even seen a story about the murders on the news there.

Mother Antonia had brought a crib and clothes for the baby Viviana was about to have, and they talked about what it meant to be a mother. Eventually Viviana began talking about her father and how much she loved him, and she showed Mother Antonia pictures of him and talked about how he spoiled her with presents. She cried as she talked about him, and Mother Antonia was relieved that she was finally letting her emotions out. Then Viviana told the story of what she had seen. Eventually she also remembered that she had heard one of the attackers call another Chico, or Chino. She wasn't sure. But more details were coming back. Soon she gave the soldiers two names, then three, then more. Then, at last, Mario emerged from his silence and gave helpful details, too.

Mother Antonia felt her primary job was to comfort the children, but she also wanted to help them remember anything that might help General Chávez solve the crime. "I am a crime fighter in my own way," she says, and she does believe victims get some measure of healing when justice is done.

Some of the men held at the ranch were eventually charged with the murders and moved to the Ensenada jail. People have asked her so many times, "How can you love people who do such things? How can you even be in the same room with them?" As she drove to the jail to visit them, she prayed that she could still find compassion for the men who had ruined Viviana's and Mario's lives.

At the jail she found about ten of them locked up together in a single large cell. They were being kept separately from the other prisoners because inmates tended to be vicious to those charged with hurting children and women. She knew many of them from the ranch. She told them that no matter what they had done, there was still hope for them because God still loved them. Then she took the men into her arms, one at a time.

"I walked out to the car alone," she says. "Tears were coming down from my eyes because I was so happy. I knew that once I choose who I love and who I don't, I am no longer God's servant."

Five years after the massacre, in 2003, we drove several hours into the interior of Baja California, through deserts and mountains to a little village where we found Linda Ramírez Bela, Viviana and Mario's grandmother. She said nobody wanted to be near her family after the massacre, except Mother Antonia, who was the only one who wanted to help. Ramírez said the massacre haunts her with "a pain that never heals," but her only comfort has been Mario and Viviana and her baby grandson.

Viviana is now a college student, with long dark hair and a pretty, soft face framing large brown eyes. When we met her in a deserted Ensenada restaurant, she smiled but didn't laugh much, very serious and very grown up. She is studying criminal law, an interest piqued by being a victim of crime. She knew that one of the men convicted of the massacre, Portillo, the ringleader, was found hanged in prison in February 2003; it was unclear whether it was suicide or murder. But Viviana said she didn't dwell on the killers or their fate, saying, "What good would it do me?"

Viviana said she had recovered from the horror better than Mario, who left school after the seventh grade. He spends most of his time now in a remote village where there is no television and no telephone service. There, amid vast expanses of cactus and scrub brush, he passes his days tending cattle and horses and trying to forget.

Viviana had never before discussed the massacre publicly, but she wanted to help out with a book about Mother Antonia. She spoke about those horrible days with no obvious emotion. When asked how often she thinks of the massacre, she answered with a cool, level gaze. "Always," she said. "All the time. Every time I close my eyes I see it all over again."

We dialed Mother Antonia's number and handed the cell phone to Viviana, who lit up when she heard Mother Antonia's voice.

"*Ay, Madre,*" she said, beaming in a way that she hadn't before.

As she talked, she giggled like a little girl.

TWELVE

THE ELEVENTH HOUR

On Mother's Day 1990, on a vast and dusty field near Chihuahua City in northern Mexico, Rome itself smiled on Mother Antonia, its most unconventional servant.

Pope John Paul II was presiding over an outdoor service for several hundred thousand people there, and Mother Antonia had been chosen to carry an offertory gift to the altar. They called her name and as it echoed across the enormous field, she climbed the steps to where the Pope was sitting. Cardinal Posadas was standing at the Pope's side, and he smiled broadly as he watched Mother Antonia approach. He crossed his hands over his chest, let out a deep sigh and said, *"Madre Antonia, hasta El Papa, hasta El Papa,"* all the way to the Pope.

Posadas meant she had come a long way from that moment a dozen years before, when she knelt in his office asking for permission to serve as a Catholic sister. When the Pope reached out and touched her cheek, it was a profound moment for Mother Antonia. The head of the Catholic Church was blessing a woman who encountered so many obstacles to serving the church that she put on a habit she had sewn herself.

As her work became more well known and her following grew larger, many told her she was welcome good news for the church. At a time when younger people were not joining religious orders and people were living longer, many in the church said her vision of encouraging older women to serve was inspired.

Then in 1991, San Diego Bishop Leo Maher, who had helped her get started, told her from his wheelchair just before he died of cancer that she should invite others to join her. "Encourage women from different walks of life, who have gifts to give, to come and give them to the poor and the sick and the suffering," he told her. Then the bishop, addressing a twice-divorced mother who had been barred by the church from receiving Communion for a quarter century, said, "Remember, Sister, you are the Church."

Tijuana Bishop Berlie was also urging

her to found a religious community. He told her that like Mother Teresa, she needed to be sure her works and spirit would continue after her death. So Mother Antonia began writing up a formal request to the church to create a religious community because she said, "I wanted to give all this joy I had to others, and I realized I must open doors for them."

In 1997, the diocese of Tijuana gave its initial consent for her to found a religious community, followed by a formal written acceptance by Bishop Rafael Romo Muñoz in 2003. She called it the Eudist Servants of the Eleventh Hour. The eleventh hour was meant to symbolize her goal of welcoming women, roughly between forty-five and sixty-five years old, to dedicate the later part of their lives to serving the poor, just as she has.

Her community is a new branch of the Eudists, an international order named after St. John Eudes, a seventeenth-century French missionary. Father John Howard, a priest at St. James Catholic Church in Solana Beach and superior of a Eudists community in San Diego, told her the idea makes sense in the face of declining membership in religious orders. According to the Center for Applied Research in the

Apostolate, at Georgetown University, the total number of Catholic religious sisters in the United States has dropped 54 percent from its peak in 1965. As a great-grandmother herself, Mother Antonia understands the million reasons why young women are less interested in joining. But she believes many older women are craving a way to serve.

Long a rebel and an innovator, she accepts people the church has resisted, those who have been widowed or divorced and those with gray hair. The poet Donald Hall once wrote about a bag he found in his grandmother's attic that was stuffed full of bits of string and marked "String too short to be saved." Mother Antonia is like Hall's grandmother: She believes everyone is useful and no one should be discarded.

She found joy and satisfaction in her own life when she dedicated herself to helping others. It is often said that happiness comes from knowing that your life matters and that others are better off because of you. Mother Antonia tells people: Want to get rid of your blues? Clean out your closet and donate those coats and shoes you haven't worn for years to someone who needs them. Visit a nursing home; bring candy to a cancer ward or to wounded soldiers in a military hospital. She also urges people to focus on the good in everything and ignore the bad. She spends her days in a relentlessly sad environment, but that's not how she sees it. She thinks it's beautiful. Her goal now is to help others do the same and to lift their lives by showing them ways to lend a hand.

Mother Antonia's community now has about a dozen sisters, and many times that number have inquired about joining, including mothers and grandmothers, divorcees and widows, doctors and nurses, Mexicans and Americans. They have raised children and buried husbands, worked in offices and in factories, and they have arrived at a point in their lives where they want to do something meaningful for others.

"I'm very healthy, and I still have something to give, but I want to give it where it matters," says Sherry Schaefer, from Omaha, Nebraska, a fifty-year-old divorced mother of six grown children, who moved to Tijuana in 2004 to work with Mother Antonia. "In so many things in my life, I got to the point where I just said, 'What for? I don't care about this.' I want to work with the poor. I want to spend my days really making a difference, because that's the only thing in my life that's giving me joy."

Schaefer, like many other women, discovered that most Catholic religious orders do not accept older people for practical reasons, including that they often find it harder to adjust to new lives, and they tend to get sick and place a financial burden on the congregation. But Mother Antonia believes there are plenty of women over forty-five who are healthy and have the time, energy, and will to help others. She prefers to have those who join her keep their bank accounts and provide as much as they can for their own expenses. "This is an order where you don't burn your bridges behind you," she says. "We want people to keep their things and money in case they have to go back to their family."

Two of the first to take their vows in the Servants of the Eleventh Hour, in 1998, were Carmen Dolores Hendrix and Olivia Fregoso. They were working in California for Rockwell International, the defense contractor, assembling parts for submarines when they first met Mother Antonia. Carmen was a widow, and Olivia had never married. They shared an interest in volunteer work, with Carmen working in a prison and Olivia in local hospitals. When they read that a Catholic sister who lived in a

Mexican prison was going to be speaking at a Catholic conference in Anaheim, near where they lived and worked, they decided to go.

"When we listened to her, we cried and laughed," Olivia says. "Something was just drawing us to this woman."

"She was like a huge ray of sunshine coming through the clouds," Carmen says.

A few weeks later, they drove to Tijuana, asking to talk to Mother Antonia when they arrived at the barbed-wire-topped walls of La Mesa. She came out, arms raised in her big, welcoming gesture, and said, "Hello! What can I do for you?" And they responded, "No, what can *we* do for *you?*"

They started spending all their weekends and vacations in Tijuana, helping Mother Antonia wherever needed, including driving from hospital to hospital one night trying to get blood for a woman who needed a transfusion. After Carmen retired, Olivia quit her job in January 1998. Carmen, sixty-five, and Olivia, fifty-four, then started coming to Tijuana nearly every day, eventually taking vows as Servants of the Eleventh Hour. They still live on the U.S. side of the border but spend their days in Tijuana. Among other things, they are the order's shuttle service, bringing donations from California into Mexico.

In late 2004, Carmen became seriously ill and moved in with her family in Irvine, California. Olivia still drives over the border nearly every day, carrying an endless stream of donated food, clothes, and other goods. Her family and friends help support her financially. "What I love is the fact that we are doing things that are really needed," she says.

Kathleen Todora was in Phoenix when she decided to join Mother Antonia. She had previously run a shelter for battered women and children and written for Catholic publications. At sixty-seven, she thought she still had many good years left and, because she had long wanted to join a religious order, she made some calls, but every order turned her down because of her age. She had just buried her mother six months after burying her husband when she read our story about Mother Antonia that appeared in *The Washington Post* in 2002. She immediately wrote Mother Antonia a letter in which she said, "If my shabby little life can be of any use to you, I would like to join you."

Mother Antonia called her, and two months later Kathleen drove to Tijuana, having given away most of her clothes and furniture. After nine months of working with Mother Antonia, using her writing and computer skills to organize Mother Antonia's lifetime of files, she took her vows. In 2004, after nearly two years in Mexico, she felt her work was complete in Tijuana and returned to Lafayette, Louisiana, where she had once lived and has many friends. The diocese welcomed her there as Sister Kathleen, and she now lives among the poor, visiting prisoners and others in need. Mother Antonia sees her as a model for others who might want to join her community, spending time first in Tijuana and then returning to their own hometown to serve.

Mother Antonia hopes to match women's skills and experience to needs in Tijuana and elsewhere, believing there is plenty and varied work to be done. Most of the sisters live at Casa Campos de San Miguel or at Casa Corazón de María, an old house in Tijuana renovated into a bright and cheery convent by volunteers from the St. James and St. Bridget Catholic parishes in suburban San Diego. Not all women who have spent decades running their own households are suited for communal convent living, and Kathleen

sees Mother Antonia as a "total noncon-
formist" who makes flexible arrangements
for anyone who wants to serve.

Lillian Manning is a sixty-three-year-old
retired nurse, a great-grandmother who
was divorced in 2000, who recently joined
Mother Antonia. When she visited the
nursing homes in her hometown of Round
Rock, Texas, she was struck by how so
many dying patients were lying there alone,
with no one to comfort them. Thinking
she could best serve them as a religious
sister, she applied to several communities,
but only Mother Antonia would accept
her. After spending time with her in
Tijuana, she plans to serve in those
nursing homes in Texas and sit with el-
derly dying patients who have no one else.

Betty Huntsbarger thought her experience working in prisons and with AIDS
patients might make her helpful to Mother
Antonia. She was so sure she wanted to
join that she put her house in Goldsboro,
North Carolina, on the market even before
she got a response from the letter she
wrote to Mother Antonia. In April 2003,
she flew to San Diego, where one of the
sisters met her at the airport. "I knew in an
instant," she said. "I felt there was a purpose for me to be here."

Betty's husband, Jim Huntsbarger, was an executive at BF Goodrich Tire Co. in Detroit who did everything for her. He paid the bills and did the taxes. When Betty needed to go somewhere, he would drive her there beforehand so she'd know the route. Betty depended on Jim's big, Type-A personality to carry her through life, but then he died and left her a forty-two-year-old widow with five children, the youngest only eight.

"We were the perfect family," she said. "We lived across the street from the school, and we were involved in the church. Suddenly it all fell apart."

She struggled to make her own way and eventually became a counselor for people with mental illness and substance abuse problems. As she neared retirement age, with her children all gone from home, she found herself asking God, "What do you want me to do?" Then she heard about Mother Antonia. She sold her house, gave her books to the public library and her furniture to her kids, and sold everything else at a garage sale. She arrived in Tijuana with some clothes and a box of family photos. Just before her sixty-fifth birthday, Betty took vows to join the Servants of the Eleventh Hour and began working in an

AIDS hospice, hospitals, and any other place in Tijuana where she was needed. "I think there's going to be a whole lot more women who are doing the same thing," she said, sitting at a table in Casa Campos in early 2004, still adjusting to wearing a stiff white veil. "I don't see life as, 'Okay, now I'm sixty-five so I don't do anything anymore.' I've got questions. I've got things I want to do.

"I think the times today call for this kind of a religious order," she said. "Raising kids, working in the world, it gives us the experience. I worked with substance abusers, and I understand what it is to be addicted. It's easier to be loving and caring when you have the understanding, when you've experienced it yourself."

It was hard for Betty, an independent woman used to making her own choices, to suddenly belong to a service order where her personal needs were considered secondary at best.

"Every time I start to complain, I hear this little voice in my head saying, 'It's not about you, Betty.' And that's really changed my whole perspective. All of my life it's been about me: what I wanted to accomplish, what I wanted to do. But when I came down here, what I hear over and over again in my heart is: This is bigger than you. It's humbling. It's exciting. I'm in on the beginning of something important."

In December 2004, a year and a half after arriving in Tijuana, Sister Elizabeth, as Betty came to be known, died suddenly of lung cancer. She was buried in Michigan alongside her husband, after a memorial service at Casa Corazón de María, where she lived.

"It meant the world to her to be with Mother Antonia," said her daughter, Deana Huntsbarger, who was with her when she died at a San Diego hospice. "She wanted to be there on the front lines bringing all her love and compassion directly to the people who needed it most. Mother Antonia gave her the chance to do that. In many ways, even though it was just for a short time, she had really found her home."

Mother Antonia knows not everyone can join her community and work full-time for the poor, but she believes many people find their life rejuvenated when they do more for others. Sam Thompson, a Christian pastor and former U.S. Marine, has seen that happen since he met Mother Antonia in

1988. He was forty-five, and after devoting his life to organized religion, he had begun to question its virtue. He had been the co-pastor of a huge evangelical church, but after he disapproved of the direction the church was taking, he was purged. He believes the church higher-ups did not want to risk division in the profitable organization. The experience soured him as he saw church leaders more interested in public image and politics than practicing what they preached.

Sam's wife, Gloria, heard Mother Antonia speak near their home in Orange, California, and told her depressed husband this was one women he needed to meet. They drove to La Mesa, and from the moment she emerged and greeted them, Sam says he's been able to put his own problems in better perspective — especially since she took him to F Tank.

It was Christmas, a couple of months after he met Mother Antonia, and Sam stood at the edge of the barbed-wire cage in La Mesa, looking at the shattered, mentally ill men wandering around in the mud and waste. He felt nauseated. Then Mother Antonia pulled up close beside him and asked, "Do you think you can do anything for this group?"

A few days later, Sam and Gloria returned with a crew of fifteen volunteers and a two-and-a-half-ton truck loaded with two large-screen TVs; sixty sleeping bags; three hundred pairs of new underwear; and socks, jeans, and sweatshirts, which they passed out in F Tank. Many of the inmates were too sick to understand what was happening. But one young man approached Sam and said, "You have no idea what you have done for us."

That was probably true, Sam thought, but he also believed that the F Tank inmates and Mother Antonia had done even more for him. "She introduced me to real poverty, and it helped me forget what had happened to me," he says.

Sam has spent a lifetime wanting to care for the poor, but he really understood how to do it only when he met Mother Antonia. She doesn't ask people why they use drugs, why they got in trouble with the police, or why they are broke and begging on the streets. She just helps, one person at a time, no questions asked.

Mother Antonia took Sam one day to Tijuana's red-light zone, where she goes regularly to check on the prostitutes. They found one woman laid up in bed with terrible sores on her feet from an infection. Mother

Antonia wanted to take her to the doctor, but she couldn't walk. So Sam, the smartly dressed, silver-haired pastor from one of America's richest counties, leaned over and scooped her up into his arms and carried her to the doctor's office. As he walked past the Tijuana cantinas with a sick prostitute in his arms, he never felt more needed.

Sam, now pastor of The Christian Life Fellowship, an interdenominational Protestant church, sends monthly donations to Mother Antonia and brings his congregation on aid missions to Tijuana. They have built four houses there, including one for a woman whose husband died trying to cross illegally into the United States.

Even as Mother Antonia's mission has taken on larger dimensions beyond the walls of La Mesa, within those walls she has had to adapt to many changes. In recent years, the Mexican government has tried to modernize the prison. The most dramatic change came when army soldiers and riot police burst into the prison in the middle of the night in August 2002 with helicopters with floodlights hovering overhead. They handcuffed two thousand prisoners and bused them fifty miles to a brand-new federal prison, easing La Mesa's over-crowding and removing many of its most violent offenders.

President Fox said the operation was designed to rein in a prison that had been out of control for many years. The next day, the government sent bulldozers into the prison to raze *El Pueblito* and its four hundred little homes and businesses, smashing dining room sets and refrigerators, couches, and stoves into a pile of twisted debris. Families were booted out. When prison officials had tried that in the past, they failed in the face of angry, violent protests. But this time, the precise, nighttime military raid caught the inmates by surprise. As we stood on the prison wall watching the heavy machinery crush decades of construction, we saw social workers lead away about forty children, many of whom carried toys and cried as they left the only home they had ever known.

For the four thousand inmates who remain in La Mesa, conjugal visits are still allowed during specific hours, but families are no longer allowed to live inside, and regular visiting hours are enforced. It is a different atmosphere, but Mother Antonia has bent with the times. She is not sure how much longer the government will allow her to stay in the prison, because every so often she hears rumblings from some prison official who believes she is an anachronism.

The new prison rules have made it harder for her to do her work. Joanie is no longer allowed to accompany her into the prison. She slept many nights on a fold-up cot in Mother Antonia's cell to help her attend to inmates and carry Mother Antonia's heavy boxes filled with donations. Now, even with a new roller-bag and help from guards, Mother Antonia is having an increasingly difficult time carrying the things she wants to bring into the prison, especially as her health continues to deteriorate.

At seventy-eight, Mother Antonia breathes heavily sometimes, which interferes with her rapid-fire storytelling. Because of her bad circulation and the chill in her cell, her hands and feet turn blue and they are cold to the touch. She has trouble climbing the prison stairs to see inmates who are being held on the second floor. Everything seems harder than it used to be. When she is especially tired she has also taken to wearing a fancy, long white nightgown to bed, in case she dies in her sleep and the guards, who have never seen her without her habit and veil, have to come get her body. She calls it her "dead in bed" nightgown.

Sometimes she thinks it might be less painful to die in La Mesa than to leave a place that has been her home since 1977, where the poor still suffer disproportionately, and where inmates still line up outside her cell door looking for a blanket or a kind word. She can't imagine leaving Mexico, her beloved second home, which welcomed her and gave her the chance to serve. When they bury her in Tijuana someday, she wants her body wrapped in the U.S., Irish, and Mexican flags.

"I wouldn't trade my cell for anyplace in the world," she says. "But every once in a while I drive by a little white house on a hill in La Jolla that has lace curtains and flowers in the front. I never think I've given up anything, but sometimes I look at that little house and wonder what it would have been like. Just to get up in the morning and go get the newspaper and have a cup of coffee and some toast. I think about playing with my grandchildren or having a garden. Sometimes when I get up at five o'clock, I'm so very tired. I wonder what it would be like to retire. But then I remember the promise I made not to leave these men and women. How could I leave them?"

Mother Antonia looks back over her prison years with no regrets and the fondest of memories. "I have not had a day of depression in twenty-seven years," she says. "I have been upset, angry, and sad, but never depressed or regretful, because I have a reason for being."

She sees unhappy people all around her and thinks it doesn't need to be that way. She says happiness is everywhere, all around us, all the time, if we choose to look for it. One day as she was making peanut butter and jelly sandwiches to take to prisoners, she paused with a puzzled look on her face.

"You know," she said, "people think what I do is so extraordinary. But look at me; what am I doing? Anyone can do it. There are so many things people can do. It doesn't have to be enormous. It's the little things. Anyone can make a sandwich."

ACKNOWLEDGMENTS

We would like to thank Mother Antonia's many friends who told us their stories and opened their homes and lives to us. We are particularly grateful to Pat Smith, who helps Mother Antonia every day, her irreplaceable organizer and our friend. Others who deserve special mention include Joanie Kenesie, who can't be mentioned enough, Norman Orth, Tom Weisman, Rick Mansur, Anita Figueredo, and Jerry Murray-Aaron. We are grateful to Carlos Bustamante and his wife, Oliva, who have devoted their lives to Mother Antonia, and to the sisters at Casa Campos — María del Carmen, Mary, Juanita, Alma, and Aisha — for their cheerful work and delicious *chilaquiles*. Very special thanks to Mother Antonia's children: Jim, Kathleen, Theresa, Carol, Tom, Elizabeth, and Anthony.

Thanks to our own families for putting up with us, especially our parents: Thomas

Jordan, who showed us all how to live, and
Nora Jordan, and Edmund and Marguerite
Sullivan. Thanks to Noreen Jordan and
Allen Reiser, Maggie and John Keaney,
Tom and Mary Ellen Jordan, Kathleen
Jordan and Paul Machle, Julie Jordan and
Jim Cummings, and Sharon Sobol Jordan
and Dave Wallace. Thanks to Thomas
Sullivan and Patricia Laughlin, and to
Francis A. Sullivan SJ, and Sister Eunice
Fitzgerald. We miss Patrick Jordan; he would
have loved this. And we wish Dorothy and
John Carroll could have been here, too.

Thanks to those who read these pages
and made them better, especially Tom
Mooney, Joel Achenbach, David Von
Drehle, David Maraniss, Ray Billings, and
Jennifer Graham. And to the incomparable
Jay Emmett: The great ones make it look
easy. Thanks to Dan Barry for leading the
way. Thanks to Bill Montgomery, Lizzie
Glazer, Richard Cockett, and Harriett
Paterson for the places to write, and to
Kim Samuel-Johnson for the heavenly days
aboard *Dance Smartly*. Thanks to Robert
and Annie Cass for the couch space, Jordi
Sales and Mary Ellen Colon for the great
food, Hugh Dellios and Cindy Johnson for
the laughs. We are grateful for the encouragement and friendship of Martha Sherrill

and Bill Powers, Katharine Weymouth, Mary Stapp, Karen Ball, Maralee Schwartz, Tim Pat Coogan, Ed Gargan, Mary Beth Sheridan, Colm and Christy O'Reilly, Paige Van Antwerp, Paolo Valentino, Robert Gulock, Grace Fromm, Kim Norgaard, Robyn Curnow, Andy Burkhardt, and Mimi Burkhardt, who died too soon. Thanks to our family at Rancho Los Charcos: Eduardo García Valseca and Jayne Marie Rager, Mom Jane Rager, and the memory of Dal Rager. Thanks to Larry and Stacey Lucchino for the hospitality, and for finally getting some pitching.

A million thank yous to our great researchers and friends: Gabriela Martínez, Bart Beeson, Mireya Olivas, and Amanda Gigler. And special thanks, as always, to Laurie Freeman.

We could not have written this book without the generous support of everyone at *The Washington Post*, especially Len Downie, Steve Coll, Phil Bennett, and David Hoffman. We are grateful for the inspiration of Ben Bradlee and Katharine Graham.

Thanks to Flip Brophy, our friend and agent, for making this happen. At The Penguin Press, thank you to the amazing Ann Godoff and to Emily Loose for her razor mind and enormous heart. Thanks also to Alexandra Lane and Tracy Locke, fellow Brunswick Dragon.

We thank Mother Antonia for what she has given us. There are no words to describe it.

And the biggest thanks of all to Kate and Tom: You make us proud and happy every minute.

ABOUT THE AUTHORS

MARY JORDAN and KEVIN SULLIVAN are foreign correspondents for *The Washington Post*. After postings in Tokyo and Mexico City they will take over the newspaper's London bureau in 2005. They won the 2003 Pulitzer Prize for international reporting for their coverage of Mexico's criminal justice system. Sullivan graduated from the University of New Hampshire and was a John S. Knight Fellow at Stanford University. Jordan graduated from Georgetown University and Columbia University's Graduate School of Journalism. She also studied Irish poetry at Trinity College in Dublin and was a Nieman Fellow at Harvard University. They are married and have two children.

The employees of Thorndike Press hope you have enjoyed this Large Print book. All our Thorndike and Wheeler Large Print titles are designed for easy reading, and all our books are made to last. Other Thorndike Press Large Print books are available at your library, through selected bookstores, or directly from us.

For information about titles, please call:

(800) 223-1244

or visit our Web site at:

www.gale.com/thorndike
www.gale.com/wheeler

To share your comments, please write:

Publisher
Thorndike Press
295 Kennedy Memorial Drive
Waterville, ME   04901